A Nonprogrammer's Guide
to Designing Instruction
for Microcomputers

A Nonprogrammer's Guide to Designing Instruction for Microcomputers

MARTIN TESSMER
Assistant Professor of Instructional Design
University of Colorado at Denver

DAVID JONASSEN
Professor of Instructional Technology
University of Colorado at Denver

DAVID C. CAVERLY
Associate Professor of Reading
Southwest Texas State University
San Marcos, Texas

1989
LIBRARIES UNLIMITED, INC.
Englewood, Colorado

LIBRARIES UNLIMITED, INC.
P.O. Box 3988
Englewood, Colorado 80155-3988

Library of Congress Cataloging-in-Publication Data

Tessmer, Martin.
    A nonprogrammer's guide to designing instruction for
microcomputers / Martin Tessmer, David Jonassen, David C. Caverly.
        xvi, 228 p. 22x28 cm.
        Bibliography: p. 221.
        Includes index.
        ISBN 0-87287-680-2
        1. Microcomputers--Programming.   I. Jonassen, David H., 1947-
II. Caverly, David C.   III. Title.
QA76.6.T4428   1989
005.26--dc20
                                                89-8099
                                                CIP

Contents

**Part 2
Programming the Basic
CAI Lesson**

**Part 3
Enhancing the Basic
CAI Lesson**

Introduction

A Nonprogrammer's Guide to Designing Instruction for Microcomputers is yet another book on designing computer-assisted instruction (CAI). We believe that it is unlike the half-dozen or more books about designing CAI that have recently been published. Most of those books claim to be "handbooks," "workbooks," or "guidebooks." However, what they do is describe characteristics of good CAI, and then direct the reader to apply the principles to designing CAI. They present valuable information and back it up with worthwhile examples, but they forget at least three important ingredients of instruction: learning guidance, practice in performing CAI design skills, and feedback about that practice. The feedback component is difficult to implement in a book. It is far easier, as we illustrate in this book, to provide in CAI.

In this book, however, we include practice and guidance as well as some feedback. We try to guide you through the analysis and design of a CAI lesson and encourage practice of each stage of analysis and design. So, we believe that this book is truly a "guidebook," in that it guides you through the process of developing CAI. The result of the design process will be a set of print screen designs which may then be converted into CAI using any computer language or authoring system. This is where the programmer comes in. A teacher or trainer who has developed a CAI lesson and converted it to screen designs can hire a programmer to convert the screen designs to a program (but more on that later).

Before we reveal our biases by stating the assumptions of the book, we should define some terminology that we use.

Lesson Components

Lesson components are displays and activities that engage the learner in a lesson. The particular combination of components will depend upon the learning outcome that the lesson is supposed to facilitate. For instance, a concept lesson must contain a minimal set of instructional components in order to facilitate concept learning, such as presentation of a definition, examples, non-examples, practice, and so on. We identify those components for each type of lesson and prescribe their order based upon the selected lesson strategy.

Lesson Strategy

When we speak of a lesson strategy, we are referring to the ways in which the lesson components listed above may be utilized in order to facilitate a given learning outcome. These strategies include deductive tutorials, inductive tutorials, drill and practice, simulations, games, and problem solving tools. Each specifies a different sequence for the lesson components.

Programming

We believe there are two types of CAI programming. The first is programming as content and lesson design, which involves specifying the lesson content and structure in screen displays. In this first type of programming, the CAI lesson is designed. The second type of programming is programming as coding, which is the more common definition of programming. It involves converting operations to program commands and executing them in the computer. In this type of programming, the CAI lesson is implemented. We assume that these two programming types are not only conceptually but realistically distinct. In other words, both types of programming can be done by the same or separate people for each CAI lesson.

Assumptions about Developing CAI

Now for the assumptions that form the rationale for the book. We should point out that these assumptions are supported by more than our biases. They are grounded in research on human learning, instructional design, and CAI. A distinct characteristic of the book is that it does not sound "researchy." We do not include references or research reviews for every recommendation, yet every recommendation is grounded in research and practice. Making the book academic would defeat its purpose.

CAI should be developed by teachers and trainers, not by programmers. In this book, we assume that teachers and trainers should design CAI. This book then is intended to facilitate CAI production by teachers or trainers who may not know how to program a computer. We believe that teachers and trainers know how to teach, and that exploiting their instructional knowledge is more important than forcing them to be programmers. The book *may* be used by teacher trainers who are also programmers, however.

Even though the quality of commercial CAI software has improved, trainers and teachers will still produce their own. There are several reasons for this:

1. As with all media, some teachers prefer to produce their own materials regardless of the quality of available software and the time required.

2. There is still a large amount of poor quality software for many content areas.

3. There are also many content areas, especially in non-school settings, where CAI is not available. A great deal of skills training, job orientation, and other forms of training are specific to the company or location, so CAI must be tailored to fit these specific needs.

4. Computers are increasingly available to teachers and trainers at all levels. Corporations are suffused with computers, which makes them a desirable delivery device for training. Employees can receive training without leaving their desks. Likewise, millions of computers are in service in the schools of America.

5. More teachers and trainers are becoming comfortable with computers and thus are willing to try developing CAI. The anxiety of computer ignorance is abating. Teachers and employees are becoming more computer literate as more of their job functions require the use of computers.

6. Programming help for CAI development is increasingly available to teachers and trainers. Students are increasingly computer literate, and therefore able and willing to code programs for teachers. Corporations regularly hire computer programmers for a variety of tasks. Why not for programming CAI?

7. The need for computer programming skills has been virtually eliminated by "authoring" programs. These are programs that prompt the user to create CAI lessons on a computer without knowing any programming language. Some authoring systems may use a very high level language that is comparatively easy to learn and use. Others simply prompt the user with questions, so that the user's answers create the

program! The more powerful authoring systems may be as complicated as a language. Authoring systems are available in different quality and price levels for every type of computer on the market. In a sense, the authoring program acts as the programming *coder* for the CAI designer.

Teachers and trainers should not have to program a computer to produce CAI; they should program lessons by designing screen displays. Better CAI is produced when the teacher or trainer can spend time on the design of the lesson on paper screen displays, which then can be given to a programmer for program coding. This allows the teacher to concentrate on the content and teaching methods of the program (although programming knowledge is helpful). Screen displays guide the teachers into a frame-based approach to software design, an approach that has been proven effective for a variety of CAI strategies. Most important, using screen displays enables the teacher or trainer to concentrate on the content and methods of the instruction, which results in higher instructional quality of the product.

Teachers should function as designers and subject matter experts of the program, not as program coders. Several CAI designers recognize that the ideal software production team in education consists of a designer, a teacher, and a programmer. However, instructional designers are not readily available to most teachers or to many trainers. On the other hand, programmers are becoming more prevalent. Therefore, it is more important that the teacher or trainer assume a designer's role rather than a coder's. This book is intended to teach the instructional design skills needed to design CAI. When the design is completed, turn it over to a programmer.

CAI should not always function as a stand-alone lesson. Teachers and trainers can incorporate software into an overall lesson plan that includes a variety of off-screen instructional or training activities. These activities may include peer consultation, worksheets, practice and testing, and teacher or trainer tutoring. Some of the most effective CAI utilizes off-screen activities. A good CAI designer first selects the strategies to achieve the outcomes and *then* decides if the strategy should be delivered by the computer or by some off-screen activity. Ironically, teachers and trainers need to be prevented from "forcing instruction into the computer" by assuming that off-screen activities are inappropriate.

Assumptions about Learning to Design CAI

Teachers and trainers learn best how to "program" CAI through a tutorial workbook approach. This approach, which we use in this book, allows the user to plan the lesson gradually through workbook exercises in each chapter of the text, and then convert the exercises directly into screen displays for final coding. A workbook requires students to immediately apply what they have learned in a chapter to their own projects, avoiding the mistake of the "now let's put it all together" approach of books that merely *describe* CAI design without *directing* one to design it. These books, as we mentioned above, require the novice to synthesize all that has been presented at the very end of the lesson or book. Some CAI design "workbooks" offer only descriptive advice with no design activities whatsoever for the reader.

To design effective CAI, teachers and trainers need to learn to apply a few basic instructional events that are matched to the learning outcome and lesson strategy. Although teachers and trainers are usually novice CAI designers, they have a repertoire of teaching techniques and strategies that they use in instruction. They need to know the essential instructional events for the given learning outcome and lesson strategy. They can embellish these with their own instructional events as they design the program. The mistake of many CAI design books is that they try to teach too many design options and factors for a single type of approach; they overload the novice with detail and options, relying on novices to figure out what they need for their lesson, or for a teacher to teach them. These books often do not allow the student to construct anything as part of the text activities, nor do they furnish any programming guidelines via job aids.

Teachers and trainers should learn that various lesson strategies and learning outcomes determine the lesson features. Teachers and trainers should learn to apply this limited set of design options to create CAI. This will enable them to embellish them more easily with their own teaching methods.

Assumptions about Program Characteristics of Effective CAI

Effective CAI design is outcome-based. The key to selecting appropriate lesson characteristics is in relating them to learning outcome(s) of that lesson. The learning outcome of a lesson determines the lesson objectives, learner readiness activities, instructional content and methods, practice and test items, and formative evaluation criteria. To classify outcomes, teachers and trainers learn to write objectives, conduct simple task analyses, and describe the characteristics of different learning outcomes.

Effective CAI embodies a microstrategy comprising instructional components that suit both the learning outcome and the lesson strategy selected by the teacher. There are five basic types of lesson strategies (deductive and inductive tutorial, game, simulation, drill and practice, problem solving tools). Each has a different set of instructional events that should be embodied in the program, depending upon the learning outcome of the instruction (concept learning, rule/principle learning, verbal information, problem solving). This actually creates a 5 by 4 matrix of types of CAI (see figure I.1). The CAI designer selects instructional events not only by learning outcomes, but also by lesson strategy.

Teachers learn lesson design best by learning how to identify the outcomes of their lesson (the most crucial step), select a lesson strategy for that outcome, and utilize the instructional events of that strategy/outcome microstrategy to design the instructional component of the lesson.

	Verbal Info	Concepts	Rules	Problem Solving
Tutorial		(MICROSTRATEGY) Definition Examples Non-examples Example classification Attribute error feedback		
Simulation				
Game				
Drill and Practice				
Problem Solving Tools				

Figure I.1. Strategy-by-outcome matrix for microstrategies, with microstrategy example for concept tutorials.

Every CAI lesson should contain an introductory "Readiness for Learning" microstrategy that encompasses two events: recall of prior knowledge and preparation for new knowledge. These elements are distinct in their definition and their effects on learning. Recall calls up prior knowledge to aid transfer and comprehension. Readiness organizes new knowledge by establishing correct expectations and structure. Readiness can be assigned to the computer or to off-screen activities.

Every lesson, regardless of outcome, should include learning strategies that facilitate the learning outcome. The learning strategies vary depending upon the information processing requirements of the learning outcome. For instance, in a verbal information lesson, recall and mnemonic strategies should be included. For concept level outcomes, analysis of key ideas, defining attributes, and generating examples may be included. Rule learning is facilitated by networking and analogies, and problem solving is aided by elaboration and metacognitive strategies. The position of these learning strategies will vary with the general lesson strategy selected.

Effective CAI can and should (when appropriate) utilize off-screen activities as part of their microstrategy events. In many cases, asking the student to consult a book, teacher, or student may be a viable part of the computer lesson (especially for problem solving outcomes that have practice and evaluation components that are difficult to design for a novice programmer). For example, readiness activities can be conducted by the instructor before students start on a lesson. In particular, research has indicated that diadic and triadic student groupings can facilitate learning and performance in computer problem solving activities, so small group lessons may be appropriate. This assumption is particularly crucial to CAI designers who are teachers, for two reasons. Experienced instructors can utilize lesson activities that they know have worked, even if they cannot be programmed into the computer. Lessons with off-screen activities can be easier to design and code than a similar stand-alone lesson that programs all activities into the computer. Once off-screen activities are legitimized as part of the overall CAI design process, teachers and trainers lose the common and harmful presupposition that computer-based instruction must all be in the computer as a stand-alone process; that using media, text, or people is "cheating."

Assumptions about the Design of Learning Activities

Explanatory feedback should be provided for correct answers as well as for incorrect ones, so that the feedback becomes more than just confirmation of success. This is because students can guess at right answers, and also make correct but not perfect answers that have some mistakes in them. Correct answer feedback is especially productive for lucky guesses, because the learners receive instruction when they are not really certain of the answer. Correct answer feedback facilitates correct but not perfect responses, so the learners can fine tune their answers and correct minor misconceptions. Certainly, different types of wrong answers should receive different types of feedback, depending on the type of wrong answer, and number of tries.

Verbal information CAI lessons should be de-emphasized. Teachers are told that verbal information lessons can be more efficiently taught outside of courseware. If verbal information is a prerequisite of intellectual skills developed in the lesson, it can be taught on or off the computer.

The Instructional Model Used in This Book

The overall model for designing CAI follows. For the lesson as a whole:

1. Choose an outcome to be taught, i.e., a course goal.

2. Identify the component outcomes that will best lead to that outcome.

3. Classify the type of learning required by each component outcome.

4. Construct a lesson map that sequences the lesson's component outcomes.

5. Assess the learner's prior knowledge.

6. Develop readiness activities that recall that prior knowledge and relate it to new knowledge.

For each component outcome of the lesson:

7. Determine the lesson components required to teach that outcome.

8. Develop on-screen or off-screen activities to present or facilitate learning of each of those lesson components.

9. Determine the lesson strategy that is most appropriate for that outcome.

10. Sequence the lesson components according to the lesson strategy.

At the course level:

11. Sequence the individual outcome lessons into a course.

12. Enhance the quality of each presentation by following screen design guidelines.

We have organized this book in such a way as to implement this design model and to follow the definitions and assumptions described earlier. It is designed to be a guidebook or workbook. The book's structure, both within the chapters and in the sequence of the chapters, is designed to enable you to follow the model using the assumptions that we have stated above.

In part 1, "Planning and Preparing the Lesson," chapter 1 presents an overview of why and how instructional design is done for CAI. Following that in chapter 1, you will learn how to:

1. determine the objectives, i.e., state learning outcomes, of a lesson;

2. conduct a learning analysis of the objective to determine the component outcomes necessary to achieve the course objective (these outcomes will be individual lesson objectives or outcomes);

3. classify the learning outcome(s) of each lesson.

Chapter 2 teaches you how to design readiness activities for each lesson by learning to:

1. assess prior knowledge of the learner;

2. design activities that recall prior knowledge in the learner;

3. prepare the learner for new knowledge using prior knowledge.

At the end of part 1, you will have identified a lesson objective (stated the learning outcome), and identified the sub-components of that lesson in a lesson map. Stating the learning outcome is important, because most of the decisions in designing CAI are based upon that outcome. Each lesson outcome will be one of these: verbal information, concept learning, rule learning, or problem solving. The lesson map that you develop will show the sequence of these single outcome lessons. You will also have conducted a learner analysis, described the learner's prior knowledge, and determined how you can use that prior knowledge as a bridge for teaching the new information.

In part 2, "Programming a Basic CAI Lesson," you will learn how to design CAI lessons for the learning outcome(s) that you have identified. This includes identifying lesson components. As we have pointed out, the required components will vary with the type of lesson outcome. The first part of each of the four chapters in part 2 guides you through the process of developing lesson components for your objectives. These lesson components include at least the following:

Objective

Definitions or descriptions

Examples or demonstrations

Learning guidance

Practice

Feedback

Learning strategies

For each lesson component, we explain why it should be done and how it should be designed, then ask you design one for yourself. In the how to do it sections, we provide numerous examples of how it ought to be done. For most components, we then provide some criteria for evaluating what you have produced.

Once you have developed lesson components for an outcome, you will need to sequence those components into one strategy. In order to do that, you will need to decide which lesson strategy best fits your outcome, content, and purpose: drill and practice, game, deductive or inductive tutorial, simulation, or problem solving tool. We provide an algorithm (a structured set of questions) to help you make that decision for each type of outcome. Each strategy prescribes a different sequence for your lesson components. So, you will sequence the lesson components required for each lesson. At the end of each of these chapters, we provide a set of criteria for evaluating your lesson or for evaluating a commercial lesson. We all decry the poor quality of CAI. What we provide in each chapter is an objective set of criteria for evaluating CAI lessons to serve as a quality control measure.

In part 3, "Enhancing the Basic CAI Lesson," we provide some guidelines and procedures for converting your lesson components into screen designs. The screen designs will be given to the programmer to encode into a programming language. Chapter 7 describes a number of guidelines on structuring the user interface, that is, making sure the student can use the lesson and that what the learner does makes sense. Chapter 8 provides guidelines on presenting information on the screen given the limitations of the CAI screen as a presentation medium. We provide screen display forms. Using chapters 7 and 8 as guides, the user will rework the lesson design practice done in part 2. The finished product will be screen displays for programming/coding into a CAI lesson.

How to Use This Book

To understand how to use this book, it is critical to understand its part structure. Part 1 should be completed in its entirety for every CAI lesson that you design. Part 2 has four chapters. Each describes the CAI features and activities for a different type of learning outcome: verbal information, concepts, rule/principle learning, and problem solving. In part 2, you should select the chapter for the learning outcome desired and focus only on that chapter. For CAI lessons with several learning outcomes, such as a lesson that has both concept and problem solving outcomes, use the different chapters to compose different parts of the same lesson. It is important to note that most lessons, based upon the learning map developed in part 1, will consist of several different outcomes and therefore several different sub-lessons (units), each of which will require a separate lesson. Consult the relevant outcome chapters in part 2 for details on how to design each of those units. Part 3 is then used to complete the lesson design work started in part 2. Using part 3, you will revise the lesson designs that developed in part 2 into screen designs which will then be coded into a computer program.

There are two primary ways of using this book: as an instructional tutorial and as a reference text.

Instructional Tutorial Approach

This book can be used as part of a formal course on designing CAI. In fact, we have formatively evaluated the text by using it in such a course. As an instructional text, this guidebook is written as a tutorial. What makes a tutorial different from standard texts is interactivity. In this book, you will interact with the text. It will present information, and ask you to respond. Completing all the workbook exercises in each chapter and then checking your responses will result in a better understanding of all types of instruction, not just CAI. For all types of learning outcomes, this text may also serve as a self-instructional guide. Teachers or trainers may work through the book and its exercises by themselves. As a tutorial, the book is adequately structured and the examples are complete enough to enable you to learn alone. Used the way it is intended to be used, it will work.

Reference-Text Approach

This guidebook is also designed to be a reference source. Information in a good reference text must be accessible. The reader must be able to find specific information on demand. A good reference text must have a consistent, well-documented structure which signals critical text information, making it easy to locate. Users would most likely want to reference information in part 2 about how to design lessons. Each of the chapters in part 2 uses the same chapter structure with roughly the same headings. These enable you to easily reference individual sections of the book, depending on the outcomes you are trying to teach. The last section on screen display design can be accessed separately for programming advice. This allows for a learn-as-needed approach to CAI courseware design. In this way, you can also use the book as a reference tool for on-the-job CAI design.

Part 1

Planning and Preparing
the Lesson

Chapter 1
Designing the CAI Lesson

Identifying the Learning Outcome
of the Lesson

Why Do It: Learning Outcomes
as Guides to Lesson Design

To plan effective and efficient CAI (computer-assisted instruction), the first step is to determine what students will learn from the lesson. That is, what do you want each student to know or to be able to do after interacting with your CAI. This we will call the *learning outcome*. Different CAI teaching strategies are used for different learning outcomes. You do not teach concepts the same way you teach problem solving strategies or facts. Therefore, it is crucial that you understand what the correct learning outcome is for a lesson, so you can design the best CAI.

How to Do It: Classifying the
Learning Outcome of the Lesson

A student may learn many things as part of the lesson, but you probably have some overall goal or purpose for the lesson. This learning outcome for the lesson can be classified into four types, each distinguished by what students learn to do upon completing the lesson:

1. *Verbal Information.* Students learn to state facts, dates, descriptions, and other forms of information. For this outcome, students learn only to *remember* and *recall* the verbal information.

   Examples: Students will learn to describe the procedure for solving long division problems.

   Students will state the definition of a noun and a verb.

2. *Concept Learning.* Students learn to correctly identify instances of some idea or concept.

   Examples: Students will identify examples of light reaction in the process of photosynthesis in plants.

   Students will identify the nouns and verbs in a complete sample sentence.

3. *Rule Using*. Students learn to apply a procedure, technique, or principle to specific types of problems.

   Examples: Students will learn how to apply the rule for long division to solve long division problems.

   Students will learn how to apply the viewing distance principle to select lettering sizes.

4. *Problem Solving*. Students learn to creatively apply various rules, procedures, techniques, or principles to solve complex problems, often where there is no single correct or incorrect answer. Note that problem solving is different from rule using in that the techniques used in problem solving are more complex.

   Examples: Students will write an introduction to a research paper, using the three rules for an introduction.

   Using the principles of time management, students will organize an efficient schedule of study activities.

For further explanation of each of these learning outcomes, refer to part 2 of this book. There, each learning outcome chapter has an introduction section discussing the characteristics of that particular learning outcome.

You Do It: Stating the Lesson Goal

Write down the overall goal for your lesson in the space provided below. What will students learn to do after completing the lesson?

Students will learn to _____

Check off which type of learning outcome is represented by this overall goal for this lesson:

_____ Verbal Information   _____ Concepts

_____ Rule Using   _____ Problem Solving

In upcoming chapters you will explore each of these learning outcomes in more depth. You will learn how to design objectives and CAI teaching strategies uniquely suited to each learning outcome. First, however, you need to identify which *sub-outcomes* must be achieved in order to learn this major learning outcome. Sub-outcomes are the subsidiary outcomes that students must learn en route to learning the lesson outcome. For instance, a novice student is not able to solve problems until he or she is able to apply a relevant set of rules. Therefore, students must learn the rules first. But before the rules are mastered, the underlying concepts must be understood. The concepts must be taught before the rules which must be taught prior to how to solve problems. This prerequisite sequence is necessary for all higher level learning outcomes. Identifying the sub-outcomes will help you fill out your lesson map, the topic of the next section.

Constructing a CAI Lesson Map

Why Do It: The Role of Lesson Maps in CAI

After the major learning outcome of the lesson has been identified, the next step is to determine what learning outcomes must be mastered in order to acquire the major learning outcome. These sub-outcomes are the instructional components of the CAI lesson, its topics and subtopics. By outlining these components into a *lesson map*, the structure and content of the CAI lesson becomes clear. A completed lesson map outlines the general scope and sequence of the lesson content. It reflects the variety of learning sub-outcomes that students must master in order to achieve the major learning outcome. This lesson map will guide the lesson design and make it easier to program an effective CAI lesson.

How to Do It: Constructing a Lesson Map through a Learning Analysis

There are three primary steps in constructing a CAI lesson map:

1. completing a learning analysis,

2. classifying the outcomes to be learned, and

3. sequencing the outcomes.

Step One: Complete the Learning Analysis

The first step in constructing a CAI lesson map is to do a learning analysis on the major learning outcome of the lesson. A learning analysis involves analyzing the major learning outcome in order to determine what sub-outcomes students must learn in the lesson to achieve that major learning outcome. This involves three steps.

Determine the major learning outcome. Write out the major learning outcome for your lesson, which you completed in the previous workbook section:

Example 1: Students will learn to arrange a weekly study schedule using the principles of time management.

Example 2: Students will learn to identify an example of light reaction in plant photosynthesis.

Determine the sub-outcomes of the major learning outcome. Ask yourself, What must students learn on the way to learning this major outcome? These are the sub-outcomes for this major outcome. For example, for a problem solving learning outcome students usually must learn rules to enable them to perform the problem solving task. This requires that rules be learned as sub-outcomes or enabling outcomes. Look at the sub-outcomes for the learning outcome in the following example:

Major Outcome:

1.0 Students will learn to arrange a weekly study schedule using the principles of time management. (Problem Solving)

Sub-outcomes:

1.1 To achieve this major outcome, students will learn to compute the number of hours they need to study each week. (Rule)

1.2 To achieve this major outcome, students will learn to classify each class into lecture or discussion types. (Concept)

1.3 To achieve this major outcome, students will learn to identify their peak study times. (Concept)

1.4 To achieve this major outcome, students will learn to distribute their study time over the week. (Rule)

In the preceding example, 1.1-1.4 are all the sub-outcomes of major outcome 1.0. These sub-outcomes are what must be learned to master the lesson objective.

Determine the subordinate outcomes for the sub-outcomes. Ask yourself, What must students learn on the way to learning these sub-outcomes? Often, there are prerequisite (subordinate) learning outcomes that students must learn in order to enable them to learn the sub-outcomes which will, in turn, enable them to learn the major learning outcome. Therefore, a sequence of lower level to higher level learning outcomes exists. In the example above, a problem solving major learning outcome requires rules to be learned as sub-outcomes. Then, these rule sub-outcomes may require concepts to be learned as subordinate outcomes, and these concept subordinate outcomes may require some type of verbal information to be learned as other subordinate outcomes. We argue that a lower to higher level approach is usually appropriate in most subject areas. A second example of this hierarchical approach follows:

Major Outcome:

1.0 Students will learn to arrange a weekly study schedule using the principles of time management. (Problem Solving)

Sub-outcomes:

1.1 To achieve this major outcome, students will learn to compute the number of hours they need to study each week. (Rule)

Subordinate Outcome:

1.11 To achieve this sub-outcome, students will identify the two-for-one notion of studying. (Concept)

1.2   To achieve this major outcome, students will learn to classify each class into lecture or discussion types. (Concept)

Subordinate Outcomes:

1.21   To achieve this subordinate outcome, students will learn to define a lecture class as one where they mainly receive information. (Verbal Information)

1.22   To achieve this subordinate outcome, students will learn to define a discussion class as one where they mainly have to produce information. (Verbal Information)

For brevity's sake, we have omitted the analysis of sub-outcomes 1.3 and 1.4, which would follow the same pattern.

This analysis of sub-skills would continue until you have broken down your major lesson outcome into the *entry skills* for your lesson. Entry skills are what you might expect students to know before they would begin your CAI lesson. You must determine some entry point for your lesson. In our example of arranging a weekly schedule, we might assume that before students begin our CAI lesson they know what "lecture" and "discussion" classes are. Thus, we would continue with our analysis of the learning outcomes until we reached this entry skill. For example, if all students did know subordinate outcome 1.21 before the lesson began, it would then be an entry skill. Entry skills do not have to be *taught* in the CAI lesson, but they must be *recalled* or *reviewed* when the lesson begins. This recall can be done during the readiness for learning activities discussed in the next chapter.

Step Two: Classify the Learning Outcomes

Review the learning analysis you have just completed, and label each sub-outcome and subordinate outcome as to the type of learning outcome (PS for problem solving, RU for rule using, C for concepts, VI for verbal information). You also may have to re-assess your major learning outcome to make sure it includes the necessary types of sub-outcomes as enabling outcomes. In the previous example we classified all the learning outcomes with these labels. In this example, rule 1.1 must be learned to master the problem solving major learning outcome, concept 1.11 must be learned master rule 1.1, and so on.

When you have completed this step, you should have a list of all the outcomes that must be learned in the lesson and the type of outcomes they are.

Step Three: Sequence the Learning Outcomes into a Lesson Map

After the learning outcomes are analyzed and classified, next you should determine the *sequence* of your CAI lesson to create your lesson map. Prescriptions that should be taken into account when determining this sequence are the *instructional sequence* and the *lesson structure*.

Instructional sequences. Each learning outcome that is subordinate in this learning analysis should be taught *prior to* the learning outcome under which it is subsumed. Since these subordinate outcomes must be learned in order to enable students to learn the sub-outcome, they should be taught as a *unit* first. A unit is defined as a part of a CAI lesson.

In our example on time management above, a unit on concept outcome 1.11 would be taught prior to a unit on rule using outcome 1.1. Similarly, verbal information outcomes 1.21 and 1.22 would be taught together prior to the unit on concept outcome 1.2.

After all the subordinate outcomes and sub-outcomes are taught, the major outcome is usually taught last. As you will see in the following chapters, each unit of the CAI lesson can also have its own readiness activities and practice exercises.

Lesson structure. Each subordinate outcome and sub-outcome should be treated as a unit within the entire CAI lesson and should be given a unit title in the menu of the CAI lesson. For example, determining the amount of study time (sub-outcome 1.1) can be the first unit of the overall CAI lesson for arranging a weekly schedule (major learning outcome 1.0). These unit titles help students keep track of changes in CAI lesson content from one outcome to another. The title for the complete CAI lesson would then reflect the content of the major lesson outcome.

To sequence learning outcomes, you would number all the outcomes of your learning analysis in the order in which the units should be taught in your CAI lesson. This can be done by grouping the outcomes.

First, number the sub-outcomes and the subordinate outcomes in a hierarchical order which indicates their relationship to one another (e.g., 1.1, 1.2, 1.21, 1.22, etc.). The sequence for the first sub-outcome for our example CAI lesson on arranging a weekly schedule would be as follows:

Last Unit in the Lesson:

1.0   Students will learn to arrange a weekly study schedule using the principles of time management. (PS)

4th Unit:

    1.1   Sub-outcome: students will learn to compute the number of hours they need to study each week. (RU)

3rd Unit:

    1.11   Students will recognize cases of the two-for-one notion of studying. (C)

2nd Unit:

    1.12   Students will compute the number of hours of classwork per week. (RU)

1st Unit:

    1.2   Sub-outcome: students will learn to classify each class into lecture or discussion types. (C)

    1.21   Students will define a lecture class as one where they mainly receive information. (VI)

    1.22   Students will define a discussion class as one where they mainly have to produce information. (VI)

Look carefully at the preceding example. Note that the major outcome is taught *last* in the lesson, since the sub-outcomes and their subordinate outcomes must be learned first. Almost every outcome has its own unit, with the exception of 1.2, 1.21, and 1.22. Why? Because 1.21 and 1.22 are verbal information outcomes that can be taught quickly, and thus can be grouped with the sub-outcome they belong to, 1.2. As a general rule, *all outcomes should have their own units*, whether they are major outcomes, sub-outcomes, or subordinate outcomes.

To identify your lesson's units, label each outcome or group of outcomes that will constitute each unit. Number the units in the sequence they will be presented to students, as we did in the example above.

When you have numbered all the outcomes of your learning analysis and organized them into units, you have completed the *lesson map* for your CAI lesson. The map should tell you what needs to be taught and how it should be sequenced.

You Do It: Creating a Lesson Map

To help you create and use a lesson map, use this flowchart. It outlines the entire process of designing a CAI lesson, using the chapters in this workbook. By following each step in this flowchart, you should be able to design a complete lesson map. This flowchart (see figure 1.1) should be referred to as you proceed through this workbook.

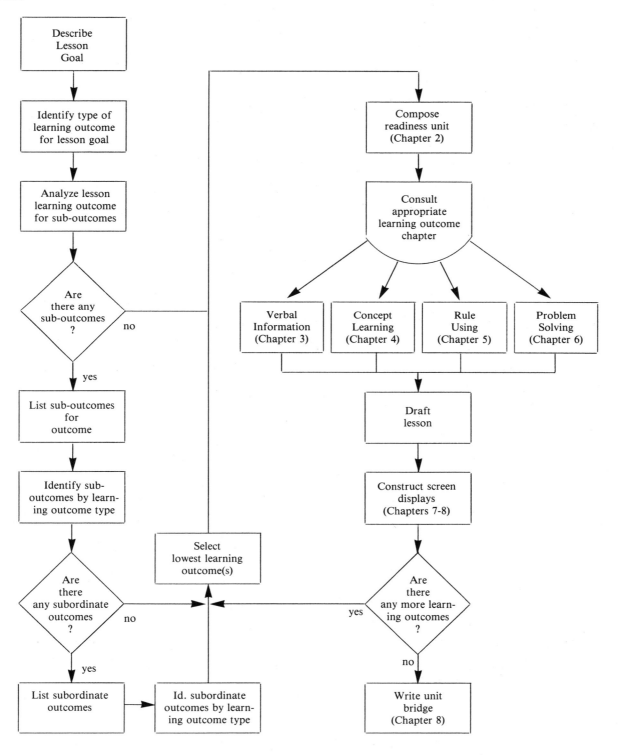

Figure 1.1. Creating the lesson map and using it with this book.

Using this flowchart, complete a learning analysis on the learning outcomes for your CAI lesson. Use the lesson outcome you identified in the last section as your major learning outcome. In the space provided write your major learning outcome, your sub-outcomes, and the requisite subordinate outcomes for your lesson. Make sure you have *classified* every outcome as a type of learning outcome. Finally, number the outcomes and group them into lesson units.

Major Outcome:

1. Students will learn to:_____

_____

Sub-outcomes:

1.1   To achieve this major outcome, students will learn to:

_____

Subordinate Outcomes:

1.11   To achieve this sub-outcome, students will learn to:

_____

1.12   To achieve this sub-outcome, students will learn to:

_____

(create additional subordinate outcomes as needed)

1.2   To achieve this major outcome, students will learn to:

_____

1.21   To achieve this sub-outcome, students will learn to:

_____

1.22   To achieve this sub-outcome, students will learn to:

_____

(create additional subordinate outcomes as needed)

1.3   To achieve this major outcome, students will learn to:

_____

1.31   To achieve this sub-outcome, students will learn to:

_____

1.32   To achieve this sub-outcome, students will learn to:

_____

Now, go back and classify each learning outcome for its type. Consider whether you have the hierarchical organization we presented in our examples. If you are not sure you have correctly identified each type of learning outcome, review the beginning part of this chapter.

Next, *sequence* this learning analysis into a lesson map of units and the order in which these units will be taught. If necessary, use additional sheets of paper.

How to Use the Learning Map to Design Your CAI Lesson

Why Do It: Using the Map as a Guide and Checklist

If you have correctly completed your learning map, you should now know what outcomes you will teach, how they are organized into units, and when you will teach each unit. The next questions might be, How do I teach them? or What instructional strategies do I use? This is where the development of the CAI lesson begins.

As you work through the rest of this book, you should use your learning map as a guide, to tell you what part of the book to use next. Based on the learning outcomes in the unit you are developing, you will use a different parts of the book. The learning map acts as both a guide and a checklist to confirm that you are including readiness, instruction, and practice elements in each CAI program unit.

How to Do It: Using the Map as a Guide and Checklist

Keep your learning map handy as you work through the chapters in part 2 of this book. These chapters discuss how each unit of your learning map will have a RIB sequence incorporated into it:

Readiness for learning activities (chapter 2);

Instruction based on the learning outcomes taught in that unit (part 2);

Bridges from one unit to the next (chapter 8).

You will need to design each unit to begin with a readiness component, to move into the learning and practice of the instructional component, and to be followed by a bridge that tells students how one unit is connected to the next. It is possible you may vary from this RIB sequence using a single readiness component at the beginning of the entire lesson, particularly if there are only a few short units in the lesson. In the end, each unit of your CAI lesson should be designed using this RIB sequence.

To develop this RIB sequence for each unit, follow the seven steps delineated below.

1. *Identify the unit.* Select the first unit of your lesson map (the unit to be taught first).

2. *Design the readiness component.* Proceed to chapter 2 and design a readiness component for that unit. If your lesson is short (1-3 brief units), the readiness for learning component may cover the entire CAI lesson.

3. *Design the instruction for the appropriate learning outcome.* Look at the first learning outcome in your unit. Select the chapter covering instruction on that outcome in part 2. Complete the design activities included in that chapter. This will produce a rough draft of the instruction for that outcome of that unit.

4. *Recycle for each learning outcome.* Repeat steps 2 and 3 above for each learning outcome in your unit.

5. *Recycle for each unit.* Repeat steps 1, 2, 3, and 4 above for each unit in your lesson map. This should provide you with a rough draft of the instruction for the entire CAI lesson.

6. *Design the bridge components.* Go to part 3 and use the techniques and principles in each chapter to design the unit bridges and the screen display sheets. This will make your lesson ready for coding into the computer.

7. *Check for RIB components.* Compare your completed lesson against your lesson map to ensure the RIB components are featured in each unit and the lesson is in a logical instructional sequence.

Once you have completed these seven steps you will be ready to begin coding the CAI lesson into a computer and formative and summative evaluation of the lesson can be started. These seven steps can also help you monitor your progress toward designing your CAI lesson.

As you move through each of these steps, you may need to backtrack to revise your learning map, or your teaching and practice routines. This is normal, greater understanding of the lesson is achieved while working through the activities in parts 2 and 3.

If this is your first CAI lesson, it will take more time than your future lessons. At the end of this workbook, you will not only have a completed CAI lesson, but you will have new-found skills in instructional design. These skills you will find useful for all types of non-computer instruction as well.

You Do It: Using Your Lesson Map with This Book

Complete the seven steps for designing a CAI lesson below. Return to these pages after you complete the appropriate sections of this book. Use additional pages for each unit.

Designing the CAI Lesson:

1. Identify the unit.

2. Design the readiness component.

3. Design instruction for appropriate learning outcome.

4. Recycle for each learning outcome.

5. Recycle for each unit.

6. Design the bridge components.

7. Check for RIB components.

Self-Check on Lesson Maps:

Have you written your major learning outcome for the entire CAI lesson?

Have you written the sub-outcomes for the major learning outcome?

Have you written the subordinate outcomes for the sub-outcomes?

Have you classified each outcome at all levels by type of learning outcome?

Have you structured sub-outcomes into separate units?

Have you created a lesson map by numbering each unit by its order of presentation in the CAI lesson?

Have you used this lesson map to proceed through the other chapters of this book?

Have you returned to these pages as you completed the other pages of the book to monitor your progress?

In upcoming chapters of this workbook, you will use your lesson map to create a rough draft of your CAI lesson. By working through the "You Do It" activities of each chapter, you will develop a complete CAI lesson ready for coding into the computer. After you complete each chapter, return to the section on using the learning map to design the lesson to review progress. The next demonstrates designing the first component of a CAI lesson. This component prepares students for new knowledge.

Chapter 2

Readiness for Learning
Preparing the Introductory Part of the CAI Lesson

Engaging Prior Knowledge in Students

Why Do It: Engaging Prior Knowledge in Students

Most theories of learning contend that the only way we are able to understand new information is to relate it to something that we already know. Therefore, we suggest that you stimulate students to engage or recall their prior knowledge that is relevant to forthcoming instruction. Prior knowledge is what students know about the subject to be taught, and includes subject-related vocabulary, skills, life experiences, or personal feelings. It provides a context for understanding the new information.

By engaging prior knowledge, students restore their background subject knowledge into their active memory. Thus, when new ideas and concepts are presented to students, they have a place to *link* the new ideas. This improves the understanding and retention of the new learning. Also, certain methods of engaging prior knowledge allow the instructor to assess if students actually have the proper background knowledge to learn the new lesson (such as an entry skills test).

How to Do It: Engaging Prior Knowledge

There are four steps involved in getting students to engage their prior knowledge for a CAI lesson: You need to:

1. determine what prior knowledge they will need to learn the new lesson;

2. identify a format you will use to engage their knowledge;

3. compose and produce an activity for engaging this knowledge; and

4. integrate this prior knowledge engagement activity into your lesson map created in the previous chapter and into the lesson.

Completing this chapter is the first part of designing your CAI lesson.

Step One: Determine Necessary Prior Knowledge

Review the learning outcomes and objectives you completed in chapter 1 of this workbook. Then, ask yourself two questions:

1. Coming into the lesson, what do students need to know already in order to learn this new lesson?

2. What experiences or background will they have to help them understand the new lesson content?

Next, make a list of what needs to be recalled by students, based upon your answers to these two questions. For example, for a lesson on arranging a weekly schedule, students will need to know:

time in class	time working
time they go to bed	time they awake
travel time to class	meal times
required activities	credit hours/classes
agenda	peak study times
massed vs. spaced practice	down study times
whether classes are lecture or discussion	

Step Two: Identify a Format and Compose and
Produce a Prior Knowledge Engagement Activity

This step of engaging students' prior knowledge can be provided by the computer, by whole class or small group discussion, by handouts, or by the instructor reviewing previous lessons. Regardless of the type of media used, the most effective means of engaging background knowledge involves students *actively responding* to questions about their subject-related background knowledge. This engagement should involve several principles:

Questions should be posed to students in a large group, small group, or individually engaging what they already know about the forthcoming subject.

Students must respond orally or in writing to the questions.

Questions can be discussion questions, problem, exercises, or essay questions.

Questions can be answered on the computer, in class, or as homework.

In order to follow these principles, several methods are frequently used. These are discussed below.

In-class discussion. One means of engaging prior knowledge is to pose questions to the class as a whole, or break the class up into small groups.

In-class example
The instructor asks students what techniques they already use when arranging their weekly schedules.

Readiness assessment. A readiness assessment is a quiz or exercise about the knowledge students should have before beginning this new lesson. This assessment is not a pretest (which covers what students *will* learn), but rather an entry skills test. This measurement can be a multiple-choice quiz or an essay, a problem or situation for students to solve, or a simple request for students to write down everything they know about the subject. It can be given through a handout, a workbook, an oral review, or even on the computer:

In-class example

Students are given a review quiz in class on massed versus spaced practice before they begin a lesson on arranging a weekly schedule.

On-screen example

```
Before we begin this lesson, let's

review some topics.  An agenda is:

        1. a list of duties;
        2. a time schedule;
        3. a writing tool.


answer?
```

Lecture reviews. While active student responding is the preferred strategy for students' engagement of prior knowledge, you might choose to use a short oral review of a previous lesson or subject before beginning a new topic. To increase the effectiveness, lecture reviews can be combined with discussions or exercises given to students.

In-class example

Here the instructor might review what was covered in a previous lesson about massed versus spaced practice to help students recall.

On-screen example

```
     Before we begin this time management

lesson, remember that an agenda is

organized by the urgency and importance

of each item on the agenda.
```

In all three of these methods, you should be attempting to get students to think about what they already know about the upcoming subject, to recall prior knowledge that is important, and to develop some anticipation for what is to come. Doing so prepares students to learn.

Step Three: Compose and Produce the Prior
Knowledge Engagement Activity

Write out all of the questions/exercises you will use for students' engagement of prior knowledge. If in-class discussion is chosen as the format, write out your discussion questions.

In-class example

(For a lesson on arranging a weekly schedule) "How do you arrange your week now?" "Are you reactive or proactive in your scheduling of your weekly activities?" "Why is it important to get into a rhythm when studying?"

If a readiness assessment is chosen as the format, create a quiz, essay, or problem solving situation. In the following example, the computer is prompting students to perform an off-screen prior knowledge engagement activity:

On-screen example

```
    Review the list of daily activities

on page 3 of your workbook, then go to

page 4 and schedule them into an 8-hour

day.
```

If a lecture review is part of this prior knowledge engagement component, a short content outline should be sketched out.

In-class example

"Before we begin our lesson on arranging a weekly schedule, I'd like to review last week when we discussed cramming for a test. In particular, I would like to review what we said about massed versus spaced practice."

In this step, we are simply asking you to compose the prior knowledge engagement activity.

Step Four: Integrate This Prior Knowledge
Engagement Activity Near the Beginning
of Your Lesson Map

Add this activity to the lesson map that you created in the previous chapter. To add it, make this activity a part of your first unit, or a separate unit that will be presented first in the lesson. For example, in our lesson map on arranging a weekly schedule, we might add an objective to engage prior knowledge for unit 1 before we went on with the lesson.

Example

1. Students will learn to arrange a weekly study schedule using the principles of time management.

    1.1   First, we will engage students' prior knowledge by performing this activity.

On-screen example

```
Take this list of daily activities

found in your workbook on page 3

and describe below how you would

schedule them into an 8-hour day.


_____
```

Adding this prior knowledge engagement activity to your lesson map expands your map and improves your CAI lesson by helping students link new knowledge to prior knowledge.

You Do It: Design Prior Knowledge Engagement Activities

Using the form on the next page, write down the central skills, concepts, or information that students should know before beginning this CAI lesson.

Students should recall: _____

_____

_____ .

    Write out the questions/exercises you will use to engage students' prior knowledge in the format just described. If an instructor's review is part of the prior knowledge engagement component, a short content outline should be sketched out. Refer to the examples on the previous pages for guidance.

Questions/exercises:

_____

_____

_____

_____

_____

_____

Content outline for instructor's review (if appropriate):

_____

_____

_____

_____

_____

_____

_____

Self-Check

Have you determined what prior knowledge students should have coming into the lesson?

Have you identified a format (in-class or on-screen) you will use to engage their knowledge?

Have you integrated this recall or prior knowledge component into your lesson map created in the previous chapter?

Have you composed and produced the means of engaging this knowledge?

Have you returned to the end of chapter 1 to monitor your progress toward designing your CAI lesson?

Preparing Students for New Knowledge

Why Do It: The Effect of Student Preparation

Once students have recalled their relevant prior knowledge, they should be given the proper mental set about the upcoming lesson. By "mental set" we mean that students need to understand the general organization of the content of the CAI lesson *before* the content is presented. Given such a mental set, students can construct a preparatory structure (i.e., framework) in their mind covering what will be learned. Recognizing both their prior knowledge on the topic and the structure of the new content, students can better organize and understand the new content as they are learning. Once you provide students with the structure and purpose of the content, they will expend less mental effort in trying to figure it out and more effort on the content itself. Furthermore, telling students about what they will learn has been shown to reduce anxiety in students who are nervous about the upcoming lesson.

How to Do It: Creating a Mental Set

There are three steps involved in preparing students for a CAI lesson: You need to:

1. determine the organization of the new knowledge they will be learning in the CAI lesson;

2. compose and produce a student preparation activity presenting this organization to students; and

3. integrate this student preparation activity into your lesson map created in the previous chapter.

*Step One: Determine the Organization
of the New Knowledge*

To perform this step, review the learning map created in the previous chapter, for the relationships between the sub-outcomes and the major learning outcome. Also, determine how the learning map relates to the course as a whole. In our example of arranging a weekly schedule, there are four rules to learn to arrange such a schedule. Each rule has subordinate concepts that must be taught prior to learning the rule. Identifying that these subordinate concepts are related to the sub-outcomes, which are in turn related to the learning outcome, is determining the organization. Moreover, understanding how other major learning outcomes such as note taking and textbook study are related to a study schedule helps students relate the various course components.

*Step Two: Compose and Produce a Student
Preparation Activity*

There are five methods you can use to create a student preparation activity:

structured overview

stating learning outcomes

preteaching vocabulary

using a glossary

pretesting or preassessing

These methods can be used alone or in conjunction with each other. Each of these methods prepares students for learning in a different way.

Structured overview. A structured overview is an outline or map of the content of the lesson. The overview may be composed of headings and subheadings or major and subordinate ideas in the lesson. The overview may also be arranged in connected prose format, in a diagram, or in a hierarchy. The value of a structured overview is that it gives students a graphic image of how the ideas will relate to each other.

To prepare a structured overview as a student preparation activity, there are three steps:

1. List the major topics or ideas that you will cover in the lesson. Do this by consulting the lesson map you completed in chapter 1. If you are going to use a glossary, the major terms may be included there as well. Try to keep the list short.

2. Choose the overview structure you think best suits the organizational pattern of the ideas.

3. Rough out the structured overview, and decide if you want the overview programmed into the computer, or given as a handout.

There are four patterns used most often, each representing a different type of relationship between the ideas in the lesson. They are illustrated below.

A *tree structure* is best for superordinate/subordinate relationships between ideas:

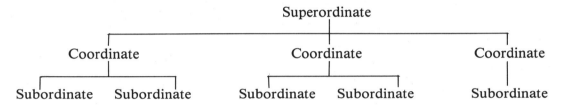

A *wheel* or *circle* pattern best represents equality relationships, where all the ideas are of equal level:

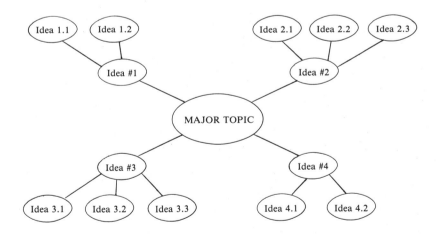

A *herringbone* pattern is effective for depicting time-order or causal relationships between the ideas:

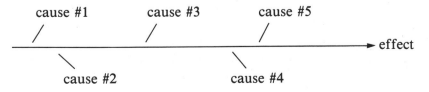

A *T* pattern is useful for demonstrating a comparison/contrast relationship between the ideas:

Concept #1	Concept #2
fact #1	opinion #1
opinion #2	fact #2
opinion #3	fact #3

Choose the appropriate structure that best represents the instructor's understanding of how the ideas are related. On a computer, a structured overview may look like one of the following:

On-screen examples

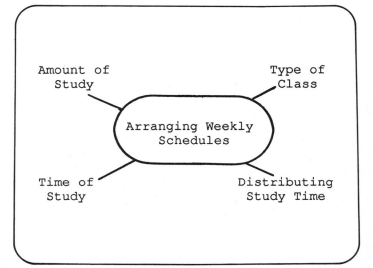

```
Arranging a Weekly Schedule

   A. Amount of Study

   B. Type of Class

   C. Time of Study

   D. Distributing
      Study Time
```

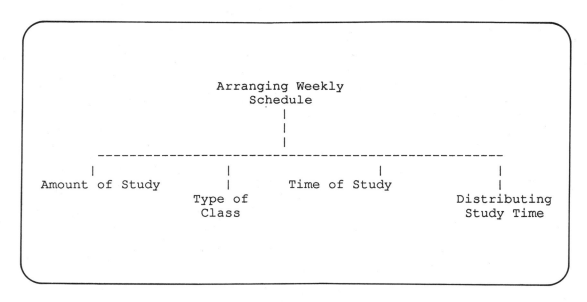

Notice how in each of these examples students should be better able to understand the overall structure of the entire CAI lesson.

Stating learning outcomes. Another means of preparing students for learning is to state the learning outcomes of the CAI lesson at the beginning of the lesson. This helps students to know what is expected of them and to focus their learning toward these outcomes. The major outcomes of the lesson should be stated as well as the sub-outcomes.

More outcome-specific information on stating these outcomes will be given later in this book. As will be demonstrated, the type of outcome you use depends in part upon the learning outcomes you are trying to develop in your lesson.

Prepare a list of the learning outcomes for the lesson as part of your introduction, following these two steps:

1. Review the learning outcomes in your lesson map to determine the major outcomes and sub-outcomes of your lesson.

2. Write these outcomes down as your learning outcomes or learning sub-outcomes in formal behavioral terms, or write them in a more "casual" format for students. The key to writing a successful learning outcome or sub-outcome is to be as accurate as possible. The outcome should *not* be a statement of content (e.g., this lesson is about arranging a weekly study schedule). Rather, the outcome should describe what students will learn to *do* after participating in the lesson (e.g., you will learn to use the four components for arranging a weekly study schedule). This is determined by the learning outcomes you outlined in your lesson map. An example of a rule learning outcome might be:

On-screen example

```
In this part of the lesson
you will learn how to determine
the number of hours you need to
study for each of your classes.
```

To learn more about writing outcomes, consult part 2 of this workbook.

Preteaching vocabulary. A third means of preparing the student for the new knowledge is to preteach the new vocabulary terms in conjunction with presenting a structured overview or stating the learning outcomes. This is particularly true when your lesson map indicates that students will have to learn a number of new terms. Teaching these new terms reduces the students' anxiety when they come across them in the lesson. It can also provide a preview for some of the important concepts students will come across in the lesson.

Preteaching vocabulary is relatively easy to prepare if you choose to deliver it through means other than the CAI lesson, since you will be doing the teaching. If you choose to include it in the CAI lesson, however, you will have to create those screens for the programmer (this will be covered in the screen display chapter later in this book). Whichever format you choose, the definitions should be as brief as possible and suited to students' reading level. Four steps are necessary when preteaching vocabulary:

1. Identify the new terms introduced in the lesson.

2. Determine whether these terms should be classified as verbal information or as a concept.

3. Decide whether you want to deliver this instruction in-class or on-screen.

    Develop a lesson using the strategies discussed in chapters 3 or 4 for learning verbal information or concepts.

On-screen example

```
One important concept you will

learn in the upcoming lesson is the

concept of lecture classes.

We will define it as:

-- a class where you primarily

   receive information
```

Since this term is a concept, you would teach it like you would other concepts. This strategy is discussed in chapter 4.

Glossary. The preteaching of vocabulary provides only one exposure to these new terms. Current research on learning vocabulary suggests that multiple exposures are necessary. Therefore, such terms should also be listed in a glossary. Such a glossary can then be accessed innumerable times to provide additional exposure to the new words for students. A short glossary can be programmed into the lesson as "help" screens. However, if the glossary is extensive, it should be used only in workbook or handout form. Since glossaries are helpful only if consulted by students throughout the lesson (thus providing multiple exposures), it needs to be readily available. The time it takes students to access an on-screen glossary, particularly if it takes them away from the context of the concept, defeats the purpose of using a glossary. Moreover, an off-screen glossary will foster transfer of learning beyond the courseware.

A glossary is relatively easy and quick to prepare if you choose not to include it in the CAI lesson, since it is used as a print handout. If you choose to include it as "help" screens, you will have to create those screens for the programmer (this will be covered in the screen display chapter). Whichever format you choose, the glossary definitions should be as brief as possible and suited to students' reading level. Therefore, two steps are necessary:

1. Determine the location for the glossary; inside or outside the computer.

2. Write out the definitions.

On-screen example

```
discussion class -- a class where you
                     must produce
                     information

lecture class -- a class where you
                 mainly receive
                 information
```

Preassessment or pretest. A preassessment or pretest might also be used to test students on the upcoming lesson content *before* they begin the lesson. Remember, we differentiate between pretests and preassessments. A *preassessment* measures whether students have the *entry skill* behaviors required by the lesson. In the example used in the previous chapter, we argued that understanding the difference between a "lecture" class and a "discussion" class was an entry skill behavior expected of students before they learned about arranging a weekly schedule. Therefore, your preassessment should measure whether students understand this difference before they begin this lesson. If they do not, then you need to either provide remedial instruction within the CAI lesson or recommend the means by which students can acquire the necessary prior knowledge.

A *pretest*, on the other hand, measures whether students already have learned some knowledge of the content *to be taught* in the current lesson. Through a pretest, students can be directed to skip certain sections of the lesson, or the entire lesson. A further benefit of pretests is that students are introduced to the learning outcomes they are expected to master. With such information, they can organize the lesson content toward learning these outcomes. That is, an effective pretest engages prior knowledge and prepares the learner for new knowledge.

Difficult pretests, however, can also have a debilitating effect on students' attitudes toward themselves and the lesson. If students are tested on content totally unfamiliar to them, they may not be able to answer any of the pretest questions. This may cause them to generate negative feelings about themselves. Thus, pretests should be used where the instructor feels that most students already know some of the lesson content. Effective pretests can be delivered and scored by the computer using random generation of test items. Students then may be branched to an appropriate starting point based upon their pretest performance.

If you use either a preassessment or a pretest, the test questions/exercises should be based on the learning outcomes or sub-outcomes in your lesson map. For example, if the learning outcome requires students to apply a rule, the questions should require students to apply that rule. If students are learning to identify an example of a concept, then the questions should offer examples for students to identify. To avoid student anxiety, a print or oral explanation should precede the preassessment or pretest. It should explain how some students may not know any questions on the test and how they should skip any completely unfamiliar questions, rather than just guessing at answers.

On-screen examples

Preassessment question

```
15. A lecture class is:

    a. a class to learn how to listen;

    b. a class that respects your needs;

    c. a receptive type of class;

    d. a discussion type of class.

          answer?
```

Pretest question

```
12. The rule for the number of hours you

    need to study for each hour of class is:

    a. one hour for every hour of class;

    b. two hours for every hour of class;

    c. three hours for every hour of class;

    d. four hours for every hour of class.

          answer?
```

Note how the questions in the two examples above are similar in style but different in content. Effective CAI lessons often incorporate both preassessment and pretest questions into one unit presented before the student begins the instructional component of the CAI lesson.

These student preparation activities can be used individually or in combination with each other to prepare students for the upcoming lesson.

Step Three: Integrating Student Preparation
Activities into the Learning Map

Since student preparation activities prepare the student for new instruction, they should be at the beginning of the CAI lesson. To do so:

1. identify the first outcome (subordinate outcome or sub-outcome) that you will be teaching in the first unit.

2. present the student preparation activity immediately *after* you have engaged the learner's prior knowledge (prior knowledge engagement activity) and *before* you present new instruction to the learner:

Student preparation after engaging prior knowledge

```
     How would you describe the

primary purpose of an agenda?

   1 announce time/place

   2 announce meeting topics

   3 describe content of
       topics.

Choose one number...
```

```
     In this lesson you will
learn to design meetings as
decision-making devices.


     You will see that an agenda
is more than a shopping list of
times or topics. It is an effective
time management device.
```

The first example screen is used to recall learners' knowledge and beliefs about agendas. The second example describes the learning objective of this unit, and explains how this new knowledge relates to learners' prior knowledge on the topic.

You Do It: Design Student Preparation Activities

If you choose to use a structured overview, sketch out the overview in the space below, following the guidelines set forth above. If the overview is to be put on the computer, remember that the computer screen is smaller than an 8½-by-11-inch sheet of paper.

Structured Overview:

(create additional sheets as needed)

If you intend to state the learning outcomes to students, the major outcome and sub-outcomes for the lesson should be written down *as the students should see them on the computer*:

Major Outcome 1.0: _____

    Sub-outcome 1.1: _____

       Subordinate Outcome 1.11: _____

    Sub-outcome 1.2: _____

(create additional outcomes as needed on separate sheets)

If you are planning to preteach the vocabulary, you should provide a list of the new vocabulary terms and a description of how you will teach them.

new vocabulary terms:

(create additional sheets as needed)

instruction to be provided:

(create additional sheets as needed)

If you are planning to provide a glossary, check whether this will be on-screen or off-screen, and create the definitions:

glossary: _____ on-screen _____ off-screen

definitions:

(create additional sheets as needed)

If you are planning to preassess or pretest students' knowledge, write the questions below in the appropriate form, following the guidelines mentioned above.

preassessment questions:

(create additional sheets as needed)

pretest questions:

(create additional sheets as needed)

Finally, add these student preparation activities to the learning map you created in the previous chapter.

Self-Check

Have you determined the overall organization of the new knowledge students will be learning in the CAI lesson?

Have you identified a method for representing this organization?

Have you composed a student preparation activity presenting this organization to students?

Have you integrated this student preparation activity into your lesson map created in the previous chapter?

Have you returned to the end of chapter 1 to monitor your progress toward designing the CAI lesson?

Summary

A complete CAI introduction should both recall prior knowledge and prepare the learner for new knowledge. Taken together, these two activities help the learner to understand the impending lesson and reduce anxiety about unknown content. There are a variety of methods for completing both activities for a CAI lesson, depending on the structure of the content and the intentions of the teacher.

Now that you have roughed out the introductory part of the CAI lesson, the next four chapters will help you compose the instructional design to "program" the entire lesson on paper, specific to the type of learning outcome in your lesson.

If this seems like a great deal of paperwork for what could be programmed on a computer, please remember that most effective CAI lessons are planned out on paper. This is similar to the production of good writing through prewriting activities. Also, when you develop this lesson map for your CAI lesson on paper, you have completed the programming logic of the CAI lesson. We will be differentiating between "programming logic" and "programming coding," which is placing the lesson into the computer via a programming language.

Part 2
Programming the Basic CAI Lesson

Chapter 3

Programming a CAI Lesson for Verbal Information Learning

Characteristics of Verbal Information

Overview

Verbal information is probably the most common outcome of the schooling process. Likewise, most professional and public service jobs are largely verbal; they involve transmitting information. In verbal learning, we state what we know or what we are aware of. Verbal learning is therefore important to the development of successful students. Piaget claimed that verbal learning and intellectual development are inextricably tied together, because the primary ways that we have of manifesting intelligent behavior are verbal. So as we are developing verbally, we are also developing intellectually.

Virtually every task for which CAI is developed requires verbalization. That does not mean that every CAI lesson should have a verbal information lesson. Often, the verbal information lessons are taught by the teacher or in a print text. Likewise, it is important to note that few CAI lessons are devoted to verbal information. Nor should they be. Verbal information by itself is seldom a meaningful outcome of instruction. However, verbal information lessons can be used as an introduction to an intellectual skills lesson, as a means to a higher end.

Having students verbally describe the skills being developed, whether they are concepts, rules, or problem solving, can be important. For example, memorizing the definition of a concept can help students identify concept examples, just as remembering a quadratic equation can help them solve quadratic (rule) problems. The information memorized helps students to master the skill to be learned.

Thus, virtually every intellectual skills lesson developed can use a prerequisite verbal information lesson which results in the ability to verbalize the concept, rule, or problem solving method being taught. So, verbal information is an important part of many skill lessons.

Definition

Verbal information may be recalled but not necessarily understood. The learner acquires knowledge of a concept, rule, principle, or procedure, but does not necessarily understand the concept, rule, or principle. Nor can we be assured that the learner can use the rule or concept even though they can say it. Verbal information refers to the *statement* of facts, rules, concepts, and so on. The statement of information is different from the use or application of the information. Having knowledge of information means only that learners can remember and state the information. It does not matter whether the information is a simple fact (such as that the capital of the United States is Washington, D.C.) or a complex principle (e.g., that people are promoted until they reach a level of incompetence). The learner may state each with ease, and yet have little understanding of either. So, verbal information can seem complex or simple. What matters is what the learner does with the information. If the learner only memorizes the information so that she or he may later state it, the outcome is verbal information. If the learner uses or applies the information (e.g., using the Doppler effect to predict the age of a supernova), the outcome is an intellectual skill, such as higher order rule learning.

Gagné, Briggs, and Wager (1988) identified three types of verbal information: labels or words, facts or propositions, and organized knowledge or summaries. Labels are the words that we use to describe things, especially concepts, such as *truth, mobility, horizon*. Facts consist of arbitrary associations between two or more labels, such as "there are 50 states in the United States," or "a decrease in price results in an increase in demand." Organized knowledge consists of the set of related facts and concepts, such as firetruck, which consists of ladders, hoses, trucks, dalmation dogs, water, insurance, and so on. This information is interrelated in a network of ideas that enables the learner to reason, draw inferences, solve problems, and so on.

Verbal Information

A person is learning verbal information when he or she can:

> Describe the procedure for making withdrawals with a bank card
>
> Recall Robert's Rule of Order regarding a quorum
>
> State the definition of *hegemony*
>
> State the symptoms of angina
>
> Know the cost of the Sunday *New York Times*
>
> Recall the quadratic formula

Behaviors That Are Not Verbal Information

> Using a bank card to make a withdrawal (rule using).
>
> Determining if a quorum exists (rule using).
>
> Identifying cases/examples of hegemony (concept learning).
>
> Predicting the effects of increased debts on hegemonistic practice (problem solving).
>
> Diagnosing angina in a patient (problem solving).
>
> Selecting a paper to read on Sunday (rules).
>
> Using the quadratic formula to solve problems (rules).

In the latter examples, the verbal information was *used* to apply a rule, solve a problem, or identify examples of a concept.

Self-Check on Knowledge of
Verbal Information

> 1.   Think of some examples of verbal information that are:
>   part of your job
>   labels for important concepts
>   facts, with one and only one possible association
>   organized, related groups of ideas

2. Check to make sure that your examples are verbal information:

    Are users simply stating or recalling the information, not applying it?

    Are users repeating existing relationships instead of generating original knowledge?

3. Check your lesson map from part 1 of this book. Did you label some concept or rule outcome as verbal information, or vice versa?

While verbal information may seem complex, the behavior exhibited is *recall*. Learners do not apply the information; they merely recall, recite, or state the information.

Lesson Components for Verbal Information

Overview

Most verbal information lessons should contain these lesson components:

the objective of the lesson,

an explanation of how the information will be used,

an organized presentation of the information to be recalled,

an explanation of how the information will be used,

learning strategies, such as mnemonics, to help the learners remember the information,

practice in recalling the information,

feedback about the practice.

In most cases, verbal information can be taught outside the computer through classroom activities or text materials. However, verbal information is used in computer lessons when the information is a *component* of a skills lesson; a unit that is a sub-outcome for a rule or concept. Normally, the verbal information lesson precedes the intellectual skills lesson. That is, first the rule or principles are taught verbally, and then the intellectual skill that will allow the learner to apply the information in the lesson is taught. For example, the instructor may first have the learners memorize the three steps in a rule and then teach them how to apply it.

In some cases, entire CAI lessons are constructed for verbal information. Why? Because there is a large amount of prerequisite information for some skills, so much so that it requires an entire lesson itself. Examples are demographic data on states or regions, chemical properties of the table of elements, or German names for household items and activities. Because of its size, the computer should only be used when the student requires numerous opportunities to review and practice the information.

For an information lesson, the lesson components may be sequenced differently in different types of lessons. However, the sequence is less varied in verbal information than it is in intellectual skills lessons, and fewer strategies can be used. Why? Because there are fewer components, and because of the simple logical processing of verbal information. That is, verbal information must be presented before it can be memorized, so inductive tutorial strategies are not applicable. Also, since verbal information can only be stated, simulations are difficult to design.

Verbal information lessons are normally not as complex and rich in components as intellectual skills lessons, such as concepts and rules. Nevertheless, a series of lesson components or microstrategies should be present in verbal information lessons.

In the next section, we describe the verbal information lesson components. In designing your own verbal information lesson, you must identify the components that you will need. Then select a lesson strategy that sequences and delivers these lesson components.

Verbal Information Objectives

*Why Do It: The Importance
of Lesson Objectives*

Introducing the outcomes of a lesson prepares the learner for the lesson, helps to recall relevant prior knowledge, helps the learner gauge the amount of effort that will be needed to complete the lesson, and provides guidelines for evaluating individual performance. These outcomes are as important to the verbal information lesson as they are for intellectual skills lessons. In this case, learners decide that they need to become aware of the information only because they will be using it in later lessons. That knowledge will dictate the strategy that the learner uses. Some indication of the future lessons that will be connected to this verbal information lesson will help the learner.

*How to Do It: Presenting the
Lesson Objective*

Describe the verbal information objective to the learner. It is important to be as specific as possible. For example, avoid "objectives" such as, "We will learn about time management." For verbal information lessons, it is also important to let the learners know that this is a verbal information lesson which precedes the intellectual skills lesson:

```
   In this unit, you will learn to state
the three steps of the Salami Principle
of time management.

In the following rule lesson, you will
learn how to use the Salami Principle
to manage your own time.
```

Explain the purpose or utility of the objective to students. Since memorization lessons can seem tedious to students, it helps to motivate them if they understand the import of the learning:

```
Memorizing these steps will help
you apply them in real-life
time management situations.

They act as a kind of "job aid"
to remind you what needs to be done.
```

In many cases, the purpose/function statement can be included in the same screen that describes lesson objectives.

You Do It: Define and State the Objectives

Write down the major objective of the verbal information lesson as the learners should see it in the lesson:

_____

_____

Include a statement of the purpose or function of the lesson:

_____

Self-Check on the Objective

Does your objective tell the learners that they will state, memorize, or recall some information?

Does your objective state the content that will be memorized or recalled?

Presenting Verbal Information

Why Do It: The Importance of
Stating the Information

Before verbal information can be remembered, it must be stated. The learners need a clear statement of the information with any relationships conveyed as clearly and explicitly as possible. Verbal information learning relies primarily on the association of one piece of information with another. So the two or more items need to be juxtaposed and the relationship between them clearly communicated. That will facilitate the association of the items.

The ways that verbal information should be presented depend upon the type of verbal information being presented. Labels may be presented differently than facts or propositions, which should be presented differently than organized bodies of information. In all cases, the learning is associative, but the nature of the associations differs.

How to Do It: Presenting the
Verbal Information

Organize the information into a menu of groups or categories from which the learner can choose a starting point. The categories should reflect a meaningful principle of organization that makes the information in that group hang together in some relationship:

```
      German Household Words

         1. activities

         2. objects

         3. features

      Choose a category to start this
      unit...
```

```
      State Capitals and Data

      Pick a region you'd like to
      learn about first:

      1. South  2. West  3. East
      4. Southwest  5. Northeast
```

Present the verbal information in an organized form. Group elements together in some form that makes sense to the student, which makes them more memorable as a group. For facts or labels a list can be subdivided. For larger bodies of information, use an overview:

```
      English        German

      sleep          schlafen
      awaken
      run
      walk
```

```
         Programming Languages

      Scientific |  Business  |  General
         Lang.   |    Lang.   |  Purpose
                 |            |
      Fortran    |  COBOL     |  Pascal
      Algol      |  RPL       |  BASIC
```

Reveal the information gradually, in logical chunks. Don't try to cram too much onto the computer screen. Give the learner time to process a bit of information, then move onto the next chunk on a separate screen:

```
English        German

sleep          schlafen
awaken         wecken
nap            Schläfchen

run
walk
```

```
English        German

sleep          schlafen
awaken         wecken
nap            Schläfchen

run
walk
jump           sprung
```

```
RAM stands for Random Access
Memory.

ROM stands for Read Only
Memory.
```

```
RAM stands for Random Access
Memory.  It stores your commands.

ROM stands for Read Only
Memory.  It contains a permanent memory.
```

Note that key ideas in the information can be highlighted to emphasize that they must be remembered.

Whenever possible, make the information as memorable as possible through the use of acronyms, imagery, rhymes, or anything that makes the important information stand out:

```
The Great Lakes are the
HOMES lakes:


Huron
Ontario
Michigan
Erie
Superior
```

```
                    (GRAPHIC)
The Cheyenne rode across
Wyoming.

Helen is a Montanan who
drove a Lincoln to
Nebraska.
                    (GRAPHIC)
```

You can also have the student generate their own images and acronyms. See "Constructing a Learning Strategy" in this chapter.

If students have to memorize a considerable amount of information, periodically schedule practice and feedback sections throughout the presentation. This allows students to fix information in memory before processing more information. Practice and feedback sequences are covered in the next section.

As students move through several screens of information, provide an opportunity to go back and review information:

```
      English       German

      house         haus
      children      kinder

      Press B to go Back.
```

```
      Output devices are printers,
      monitors, voice synthesizers.

         (GRAPHIC)

      Press R to review previous
      computer components.
```

If students can go back and review information, they can compare it to the new information they are previewing, enabling them to better integrate both types of information into memory. They can go back to the previous screen or to a previous section.

You Do It: Compose a Verbal
Information Presentation

For each of the verbal information objectives in your lesson, take a sheet of paper and demonstrate how you would present the information to students. As we have just seen, there are a variety of ways to present verbal information. The important thing is to organize the display. Use tables or charts whenever possible to display verbal information. For more complex bodies of information, you may want to use figures or tables.

Screen Sequence 1 (screens on first chunk or section of information):

Screen Sequence 2 (screens that elaborate upon or add to first screens' information):

Self-Check on Information Presentation

Is the information presented in a group or sequence that makes it easier to learn and recall?

Is the information presented in small chunks for easy learning?

Have graphics, illustrations, etc., been used to make it memorable?

Providing Practice for the Learner

*Why Do It: The Importance
of Practice*

Practice is important for learning verbal information as well as intellectual skills. Practice in remembering may not be as complex as practice in applying rules or in problem solving, but it is nevertheless important. Through practice, students evaluate how well they have memorized the information. Practice also allows students periodically to retrieve information from memory, which improves students' information recall capabilities.

*How to Do It: Designing
Practice for Recall*

The primary strategy for practicing verbal information recall is rehearsal, repeating the information over and over. The amount of information that is practiced at a time is an important issue.
You may ask the learners to recall one idea at a time.

> The German word
>
> for sleep is _____.

Multiple choice or fill-in answers can be used. However, multiple choice answers may allow for more guessing.

For larger amounts of information, have students recall an organized body of information. To do this, they can complete a table or outline:

```
Name of    Type of    Sense of   Sense of   Feeds on   Environment
Mammal     Limbs      Smell      Sight      What?      Lives in
------------------------------------------------------------------
Monkey
Bear
Shrew
Cow
Lion
```

You can also provide *cues* or *helps* for students who have trouble remembering:

```
    The German word for
    house is H _ _ _.
```

```
The German word for sleep
is _____.

Type in answer & RETURN.
Press H for HINT before
answering.
```

The first example contains a cue as part of the question, while the second provides it as an option. As students practice, hints can be removed from the program. Cues are especially useful if students have later opportunities to recall the information without cues, as in a game, drill, or test.

Where students have to learn a substantial amount of information, schedule practice periodically throughout the unit/lesson. Present a group of 4-6 items, then follow it with short practice, then repeat the sequence for more items, etc.

You Do It: Develop Verbal
Information Practice Exercises

On a separate sheet of paper, design practice exercises for each of the objectives. If you used a table or some form of organized presentation to present the verbal information, start by using the same table form (though empty) to present the practice. Additional practice items may not use the table or may use a different configuration to add complexity to the task. However, the initial practice item ought to use the same form as the presentation.

Screen Sequence 1 (initial recall practice with tables/cues):

Screen Sequence 2 (additional practice items):

Self-Check on Practice

Have you included practice for every verbal information item?

Have you scheduled periodic reviews of practice items?

Providing Feedback to the Learner

*Why Do It: Feedback as
Reinforcement*

Feedback is one of the most important instructional components in a lesson. It is often said that the examples and the feedback do most of the teaching. Practice is important, but knowing the accuracy of the performance is an essential part of that process. Feedback may serve a variety of functions, however.

In different learning situations, feedback may play a variety of roles. Feedback may confirm a correct answer; it may provide knowledge of results (how well the learner performed). Feedback may also be instructional, providing an explanation of the answer. Feedback may also be diagnostic, providing corrective information to the learner based upon the learner's specific type of mistake. In higher order learning activities such as concept or rule learning, feedback frequently plays an instructional and diagnostic role. For verbal information learning, feedback more often presents the correct answer or tells the learners if they were correct or not. However, verbal information feedback can also be more artfully designed. It can cue the learner, elaborate upon correct responses, and provide summary performance reports.

*How to Do It: Designing Feedback
for Verbal Information*

For correct answers, provide the students with some confirmation that they are right. This should be done in as interesting a way as possible, through the use of humor or graphics:

```
Gut! Gut! Sehr gut!

  The word for house is
haus!!

  Don't forget, haus
also sounds like "house."
```

```
        (AWARD GRAPHIC)

Your answer: Cheyenne

  Right!! Remember: the
Cheyenne rode across Wyoming.

  Did you know: Wyoming is the
home of Yellowstone & Teton
parks??
```

In the first and second example, some additional information has been added as a part of the feedback. The second example provides a quick reminder of the recall mnemonic. The point is that correct answer feedback can be used to motivate, inform, and explain.

For incorrect answers, a variety of messages can be given, depending on the type of incorrect answers. For "near miss" answers, a cue about the nature of the miss should be given, not the answer. For other answers, a stronger cue can be given:

```
Your answer: haas

  Close but no cigar!

You've misspelled the word.
Try again.
```

```
Your answer: kinder

  No. The word sounds like
"house."

  We'll try this one again
later.
```

Whenever possible, avoid *giving* the students the correct answer on a first miss. Have them try again. Note that in the second example students try the problem later in the program, while in the first example they try it again immediately.

You Do It: Construct Feedback Messages

Take each of the practice exercises developed, and design a series of feedback messages for it. Include feedback for correct answers, incorrect answers (wrong first time), and second/third try misses. Decide if you will send students back to the same exercise immediately, back to it later on, or just to another problem.

Screen Sequence 1 (correct answer messages for first and successive tries):

Screen Sequence 2 (cue/hint feedback for "near" and "far" errors):

Self-Check on Feedback

Has feedback been provided for right and wrong answers?

Does wrong answer feedback vary with the type of mistake made?

Do students repeat practice on items they miss?

Learning Strategies to Facilitate Verbal Information Learning

Why Do It: Facilitating Recall of Verbal Information

Since verbal information learning is the most commonly practiced in schools, many learners have acquired skills for cramming information into memory so that it may be recalled later. Often, the strategies that students use to recall information are not the most productive. The most common strategy they use is brute force rehearsal, which follows the rule "keep repeating the information over and over until it is committed to memory." To remedy this problem, a number of learning strategies are available to help learners better memorize information.

Learning strategies, as we point out in other chapters, are different from practice. Practice aids recall of specific information. Learning strategies are skills that can be used to memorize different information. Learning strategies help the student learn how to learn. Even though verbal information learning does not require as deep processing as higher order intellectual skills, it can still be difficult to remember things, especially large bodies of information. Learning strategies may be used to help a learner remember all verbal information, that is, to acquire verbal information skills. Most important, these strategies can be embedded into the computer lesson.

How to Do It: Embedding Verbal Information Strategies in CAI

Most verbal information learning strategies help the learner to organize the information to be recalled, or use imagery to make it more memorable. A fundamental principle of memory is that if the information is not organized when it is memorized, it will be more difficult to retrieve that information from memory. Some verbal information strategies also use elements of prior knowledge to aid in remembering verbal items.

Verbal or image mediators. When learning labels, one is often learning arbitrary associations between a word that has meaning and another word that does not. The learner wants to form a link between them. Thus, it is possible to use a verbal or image mediator. The verbal mediators work best if they look or sound like the word being learned.

If the words have no natural verbal connection between them, have the learners *create* an image from the new word. For instance, the German word for *to increase* is *zunehmen*. That looks/sounds like *zuni men*. Think of native Americans who are increasing in numbers. There is the link. These mediators can be suggested in the CAI, or learners can generate their own:

```
          The German word for "increase"

             is zunehmen ("zuni-men")

          What image does this word call

                    to mind??
```

Acronyms. Perhaps the most common mnemonic strategy is an acronym. An acronym is a word or nonsense word in which the letters represent a word, usually the first letter in a word. Common examples of acronyms include:

STAB for the voices in a quartet: *s*oprano, *t*enor, *a*lto, *b*ass

HOMES for the Great Lakes: *H*uron, *O*ntario, *M*ichigan, *E*rie, *S*uperior

Acronyms are useful as long as the information does not have to be learned in a specific sequence contrary to the order of the acronym.

Graphic organizers. In presenting bodies of knowledge, students may complete a table or figure. For organized bodies of knowledge, we showed a tree arrangement of the ideas, which depicts the organization of the information. As a strategy, use the same tree again in the lesson, with blanks for learners to fill in.

```
                              Minerals

                      _____        Stones

  _____   Common      _____   _____   Masonry

  _____   Aluminum   _____   Sapphire      _____

  Silver      _____  Brass        _____    Granite

  _____  _____  _____   _____   _____
```

There are numerous other mnemonic and organizational learning strategies. All may be used to productively facilitate verbal information learning.

You Do It: Construct a Learning Strategy

Go back and review the presentation components of the verbal information unit. Wherever information is presented, determine if some memorable acronym, image, or saying can be used. Decide if you want to *give* the student the memorable tactic, or have them generate their own via a learning strategy. For each one they will generate, rework the original presentation to incorporate a learning strategy:

Screen Sequence 1 (screens with acronyms or images):

Screen Sequence 2 (screens with information organization activities):

Screen Sequence 3 (screens with sayings, verbal mediators, etc.):

Self-Check on Learning Strategies

Do all verbal information items have a learning strategy?

Will students know how to use the strategy correctly?

Selecting a Lesson Strategy

Why Do It: Lesson Strategies for Different Instructional Purposes

Different learning outcomes require different information processing. That processing will be used in different settings, which suggests even more varied approaches to teaching.

Concepts, rules, and problem solving may employ a variety of lesson strategies. However, verbal information learning can only be facilitated by drill and practice and game strategies, or a deductive tutorial. There is no such thing as an inductive tutorial for recall of verbal information. Having students induce facts is more inefficient and ineffective than telling them the facts via deductive tutorial. Similarly, verbal information simulations are rarely used, since simulations require the application of *skills*, not facts. Games and drills can be used to enhance information recall, since they are variations on basic practice routines. They can be used for any type of outcome.

To select the proper strategy for the verbal information unit or lesson, answer the questions below:

Step 1.   Have students already memorized the information you want them to recall, and are they ready to practice it?

If they have not yet memorized it, go to step 2.

If they have memorized it and are ready to practice, go to step 3.

Step 2.   You need to construct a deductive tutorial. Go to "Tutorials" in this chapter.

Step 3.   Do you want to motivate students by making the practice competitive and challenging?

For competition and challenge elements, go to "Games" in this chapter.

For regular practice, go to the "Drill and Practice" in this chapter.

CAI Lesson Strategies

Tutorials

Why Do It: Tutorials for
Learning Information

As we stated earlier, verbal information is frequently learned outside of the computer, through live classroom instruction or text-based materials. In some cases, however, it may be more suitable for the computer to teach students information. In cases where the information is a sub-outcome of a larger skills lesson on the computer, the information tutorial can be a unit of a computer lesson, with its own instruction and practice components. In this way all of the necessary instruction is in the same program. In cases where there is a large amount of information to be learned, the computer tutorial can provide numerous opportunities for review and practice of content.

Of all the information teaching strategies, tutorials are the best at *teaching* the student new content. Games and drills provide recall practice to *enhance* information that has already been learned, but do not teach new information. Through the tutorial, a student is given new information in an organized and memorable fashion, with opportunities for practice and feedback. The tutorial acts as a tutor would, teaching and monitoring the student through the lesson.

How to Do It: Constructing a
Deductive Tutorial

To construct an information tutorial, complete "Lesson Components for Verbal Information" in this chapter. Overall, the tutorial must contain a presentation and a practice/feedback sequence of screens. More specifically, it should:

1.   Introduce the objective and purpose of the lesson.

2.   Present information in organized and memorable "chunks."

3.   Utilize mnemonics or imagery to enhance memorability.

4.   Incorporate learning strategies to aid processing and recall.

5.   Present spaced practice or review of content.

6. Present diagnostic and informative feedback for practice.

7. Branch students to see new content, repeat missed questions, and access help.

The practice segments can also incorporate elements of games or drills. That is, the practice can be completed as a drill or game or it can be added after a short practice component as an enhancement to the tutorial.

You Do It: Construct a
Deductive Tutorial

Return to the lesson components section and follow each of the steps of the segments on how to do it and activities/steps to follow. Make sure that you do not cram too much information into your presentation and practice screens. Dole out the information in small "bites" and elicit practice in the same manner.

Screen Sequence 1 (see lesson components on objectives, purpose):

Screen Sequence 2 (see lesson components on presenting information):

Screen Sequence 3 (etc.):

Games

Why Do It: Games for Learning
Bodies of Information

One of the quintessential learning problems with verbal information is boredom. If students must learn large bodies of verbal information in a lesson (e.g., the capitals of the 50 states), they have problems motivating themselves to memorize the information. In response to this problem, game strategies can be the most interesting and motivating of all computer strategies for verbal information.

Games can incorporate elements of competition and challenge to make recall exercises more interesting. Through the use of graphics and sound, the lesson becomes more captivating. By using an awards or achievement system for game players, students concentrate more on the memory task at hand. In many cases, the game can be incorporated as a followup to a tutorial, since students can receive extra practice through use of a game.

How to Do It: Games for
Extensive Information

Games are most suitable for larger bodies of information, since small amounts of information can be easily learned off-screen, or as part of a short tutorial. The information can be part of a unit that teaches a sub-outcome for a larger lesson on skills, or it can be an independent lesson in itself.

Describe the objective and purpose of the lesson. Give students the directions and rules for the game:

```
          (MAP)

   The States Game

    The object of this game
  is to get from New York
  to California via the
  shortest route possible.

  To do this you must name
  the capital of each state
  you will travel through.
```

```
          (GRAPHIC)

   Living with German

    In this game you will have to
  name each household item that
  you encounter in each room of
  the house.

  The object of the game is to
  get out of the house by going
  through all the rooms. You must
  name 3 objects in each room.
```

Present a game item that requires recall of information. Students may choose an answer or type in their own. For short answers, typing in their own is recommended, since it prevents guessing:

```
       (MAP)


  You have chosen to start
  with New Jersey. Its capital
  is:

  a. Trenton      b. Austin

  c. Camden      d. Hartford
```

```
    pts. 0         tries 0

       (House Graphic)

  The German word for house

     is: _____
```

If students type in answers, it will be necessary to decide if misspellings, lack of capitalization, etc., should be accepted as correct answers.

Provide students with feedback on their performance and status in the game. As indicated in the lesson components section on practice and feedback, students may repeat the question, and be cued about the correct answer:

```
    (MAP)

Correct! Now you're out
of Missouri!!

Pick your next state.
```

```
    pts.  0    tries 1

Not quite. The word for
house sounds like "house."

RETURN to try again....
Space Bar for next problem....
```

In the second example, students have the option of choosing to repeat the game question, or selecting another one.

Continue the game questions until some logical end point is reached. The end can be when a certain number of questions have been tried, an achievement level is reached, or when the student elects to end the game. In any case, provide a summary of student results at the end:

```
Very good! You made it to
California by going thru
14 states.

There is a quicker way,
however. Would you like
to try again?

RETURN to try again....
Space Bar to end game....
```

```
    Score 105    Tries 12
Congratulations! You made it
through the house!!

11 tries or fewer = Native
12-15 tries       = Tourist
15 tries or more  = Get a
                    guide!!
```

There are several other features that can be incorporated into a verbal information game to make it appealing and instructive:

use graphics whenever possible to liven up the screen presentation.

for some games, groups of 2-3 students can play the game together. Students can provide feedback and guidance to each other, and have fun.

allow students some way to exit a game before the game is over. By doing this, students will not feel "trapped" in the game. See part 3 on screen design.

Drill and Practice Routines

Why Do It: Drills for Frequent
Recall Practice

Like games, drills are best suited for larger bodies of verbal information. Drills provide frequent and repetitive practice in recalling facts, definitions, and statements. They can be used to practice verbal information sub-outcomes for a lesson on concepts, rules, or problem solving. They can also be used as an extension of a tutorial, to provide more practice and feedback for recall.

The strength of computer drills is that: (1) students cannot "sneak a peek" at the answers (which is tempting to do in recall practice) and (2) students receive diagnostic feedback about the *types* of recall errors they make. If the drill does not have special feedback routines, it loses its value as a computer lesson, and might just as well be put on paper.

How to Do It: Using Practice
and Feedback Strategies
in the Drill

At their simplest, drills are simple question and answer routines. However, there are several presentation and feedback strategies that can make a drill more effective. These are outlined in the following procedures.

Begin with a statement of the objectives, purpose, or function of the drill. Since verbal information drills may seem especially tedious to some students, it especially helps to explain the benefits of the drill:

```
         Grammar Rules Review

  In this unit, you will review
  the basic punctuation rules
  used to write sentences.

  Memorizing these rules will
  help you master the second
  unit of this lesson, using
  punctuation in sentences.
```

Note that this lesson only deals with the *recall* of a set of grammar rules, not their *application*. This unit teaches a verbal information sub-outcome for the rule learning outcome of the lesson.

Present the first drill problem. Normally, it is a good idea to make the first problem an easy one for the students, to get them into the flow of the practice routine. The problem can be multiple choice, or open answer:

```
Problem: 1      # Correct: 0

A period is used:

a. at the end of a sentence.
b. at the beginning of a word.
c. between two clauses.
d. at the beginning of a list.
```

```
Problem: 1      # Correct: 0
A period is used at the
_____ of a _____.


Type in the two words that
best complete this sentence.
```

For student self-assessment, it helps to give the students a running tally of their drill progress, as indicated in these examples.

Provide feedback for student responses. The most basic response is a simple "right" or "wrong." The best feedback is *diagnostic* feedback, where different feedback messages are constructed for the different types of errors made:

```
Your answer: at the end of a
sentence.

Very good! Periods are mainly
used to end a sentence, since
they signal a completed thought.

Press RETURN for a new question.
```

```
Your answer: at the end of a
clause.


Not quite. Periods indicate the
end of a complete thought.

Press RETURN for new question.
Space Bar to try again.
```

To enhance recall, a good drill should allow students to repeat a drill item that they missed, with or without cueing. Confirmatory feedback that elaborates upon their answers and/or reminds them of the correct answer characteristics can be designed for correct answers.

Branch students to the appropriate follow-up screen. If students correctly answer the drill item, they can go to the next. However, if they have missed the item, they can be sent back immediately to repeat the item, or they can repeat it later:

```
          Not quite. Periods indicate the
          end of a complete thought.

          Keep this in mind. You will get
          this question again later on.
```

If the students' second try at the question is likely to be correct, consider giving them the problem later on in the drill. Otherwise, the question can be immediately repeated.

Repeat the drill, feedback, and follow-up procedures until the pool of drill items is completed. At that time, provide the students with a summary screen that details their performance on the drill:

```
          You have correctly answered
          40% of your questions on the
          first try.

          35% on the second.
```

For drills with a large number of questions, this summary screen can be shown whenever the student exits the drill, even if the drill is not complete.

There are several other features that can be built into the drill, depending upon the lesson content and purposes:

For drills with a large amount of items, randomize the order of items presented. That is, the computer will choose drill items at random to present them to the student, so no two students get the same drill.

Use graphics in the drill whenever possible. Pictures of the terms or subjects of questions are interesting, and feedback can be graphically reinforced as well.

Have the computer program record each student's performance on each drill item, which can then be accessed by the teacher to evaluate student performance.

Where drill items vary in difficulty, group items into difficulty levels (easy, hard, tough), and let students choose a level at the beginning of the lesson.

You Do It: Construct an Information Drill

Beginning with introductory drill screens, outline a drill and practice routine on paper. Construct all practice items first, then develop the branching strategies for all possible answers, and finally the feedback for each type of answer. Branching and feedback information can be contained on the same screen.

Screen Sequence 1 (objectives, purpose, directions, menu):

Screen Sequence 2 (drill items for each piece of information):

Screen Sequence 3 (branching strategies for each anticipated answer, including unanticipated answers):

Screen Sequence 4 (feedback for each answer/attempt and summary scores):

Using Database Management Tools to Aid
Verbal Information Learning

Why Do It: Databases as
Organizational Aids

Database management systems are software packages that help users organize information. A database management system consists of a series of programs that help users manage information. A database represents a body of information and its structure. It is arranged in a grid, with information organized into records and fields.

A record is an individual instance or entry in the database, such as a record for an employee, or a part in an inventory. Each record is broken down into consistent sections or fields. For instance, the first field in a record on an employee may contain the employee's name, the second field the address, the third the department, and so on:

(Field 1) Name: Mary Butler

(Field 2) Address: 2365 Bell Court, Middletown

(Field 3) Department: Hydraulics; General Dynamics Corp.

This structuring of data or information in the database enables the computer to quickly search for records or rearrange database information.

While database management systems are most often used in businesses to organize employee records, orders, parts information, and the like, they may also be used to help learners organize information for learning. They are useful where the learner must absorb large bodies of organized inforamtion, such as the names, uses, and characteristics of vitamins.

Databases can be created by the instructor for students to use, or students can create their own databases from information given. Using and creating databases forces learners to organize bodies of information that they are trying to learn. That makes the verbal information more memorable. The organization of the information is facilitated by the database management system. The system fosters thinking in a way known as a *learning strategy*. Learning strategies are mental operations that facilitate learning. That is, they help learners to acquire different kinds of knowledge, skills, or performance. For instance, if learners were studying vitamins, they may want to use a cross-classification strategy, where each type of vitamin comprises a record and its uses and characteristics are fields. This partial database would contain all of the factual information about vitamins in an organized fashion, which makes it more memorable.

How to Do It: Creating a
Database Tool

Determine if a database tool will help your learners. Do they have to learn a large amount of information? Can the information be organized into sub-categories or fields? If the answer to both of these questions is yes, a database tool can be useful.

Decide if you will create the database for students to use, or you will have them create their own database, or both. If you intend to use the database as a reference or help tool, you can create the database. If you want students to practice organizing the information have them create one or fill in the gaps.

```
Vitamin: K

Name: phytomenadione

Physiology: liver functions
             blood clotting

Therapeutic: bleeding, anticoagulant
```

```
Complete the following information:

Vitamin: K

Name: _____

Physiology: _____

Therapeutic: _____
```

You can also have students view or reference a database during the lesson, and then construct their own as a practice task.

Determine if the database will be used as a help or reference tool for your lesson, or as a drill or review. When you create a database, students should be able to call it up during the lesson, as a review tool. If they are to construct one, this can be done after the lesson (as a final review), or during the lesson (as a review task before moving onto more information).

```
   The next set of vitamins to
study are the nontoxic
vitamins.

Press "R" to review toxic vits.

Press RETURN to go on.
```

```
   The next set of vitamins will
be the nontoxic vitamins, ones
that have no adverse effects.

   Before we look at the nontoxic
vitamins, let's see what you
remember about toxic vitamins.

Press RETURN to make database.
```

The first example shows the database, the second has it constructed. As we said, both features can be combined in the same lesson.

If you are using a database as a help or reference tool, the student can browse through the information or search for specific instances. This is what databases do best. They permit learners to search for specific instances of information in a certain field, or to look for combinations.

```
You pressed RETURN to review toxic
vitamins. What would you like to see??

     1 Toxic vitamins in foods?
     2 Soluble and insoluble types?
     3 Toxicity levels?
     4 Other

Enter number of your choice and RETURN.
```

There are a number of options that you can use with a database to improve its learning effectiveness:

If you provide a database, have learners rearrange the database into new fields or records, to encourage them to actively process the information you gave.

If students are constructing their own database, have them complete one field first (for all records), and then move to another field.

Where students will construct or complete a database, set the computer to record all students' database input. The database record can then be printed out to evaluate.

You Do It: Construct a Database

If the amount and structure of the information lesson is suitable, construct a database tool or exercise for the student to use:

Screen Sequence 1 (displays of database information on the computer):

Screen Sequence 2 (student practice or activities using database):

Screen Sequence 3 (screens that announce or guide students when they use the database. This can include rewriting lesson screens to include a "review" or "help" command to see the database):

Summary

Much of verbal information is taught and learned outside of a computer, since computers are better utilized for skills learning. However, verbal information is an important sub-component of many skills lessons, and can be effectively incorporated as a unit of a larger lesson. The key to the design of an information lesson is to make the verbal information as memorable as possible, and to provide for ample practice and review. Deductive tutorials are used to present new information and provide practice, while drills and games are used to provide more motivating or extensive practice.

For many of you who read this chapter, verbal information is a sub-outcome of your lesson, one of the sub-outcomes of your lesson map. In that case, verbal information is part of a lesson that also teaches concepts, rules, or problem solving. Thus, you will want to consult one of the next three chapters to design instruction for the next outcome on your learning map. Do not forget to design a "bridge" screen or two that will tell learners when they have moved from a unit on the verbal information outcome to a unit on a skills outcome.

Chapter 4

Programming a CAI Lesson
for Concept Learning

Characteristics of Concepts
and Concept Learning

Overview

Concepts are all around us. They are a part of our academic and everyday world. Concepts are the names that we give to classes of objects, events, or activities. They are the ideas that we have, and as such are a large part of our intellectual makeup. These concepts are ideas that contain the descriptions of things, or their defining attributes. A concept of a dog is our idea of a dog; the characteristics enable us to recognize a dog when we see one.

Concepts help us to describe things, to relate them to other things and to tell if two things are the same or different. Concepts are also the building blocks for higher order intellectual skills such as rules (principles) and problem solving skills, which are discussed in the next two chapters.

Definition

A concept describes a class or group of objects, events, or activities. Inclusion of an instance into the concept class is based upon the instance having the defining characteristics of that concept. The defining characteristics may be sensory qualities such as the appearance or sound of something, but they may also be symbolic characteristics. A definition of "justice" or "positive reinforcement" would have abstract defining characteristics. Some of the defining attributes of the concept "bluejay" are visual and concrete.

Concepts

A person has grasped a concept when he or she can:

Identify a dog as a dog on the basis of its distinguishing attributes (has a tail, four legs, barks, etc.).

Tell that a certain building is an example of Gothic Revival architecture.

Tell if a given text is a serial publication or not, based on the definition of serial.

Classify instances of classroom behavior as cases of positive reinforcement, negative reinforcement, or punishment. This involves knowing three concepts, and being able to tell them apart.

Learned Behaviors That Are Not Concepts

Knowing how to calculate the average of a series of numbers (this is rule learning).

Being able to state the definition of "dog" (this is simple memorization of verbal information).

Labeling both serials and monographs as "serials" (a person who correctly learns a concept must be able to tell examples from non-examples of the concept).

Self-Check on Knowledge of Concepts

Think of some personal examples of concepts:

Can you think of concepts that are part of your job?

In your home, what concepts do you use to identify household items, and to conduct household activities?

What are some concepts that are currently in the news, or in current events (such as the concept of super-conductivity)?

Check to make sure that each of these are really concepts:

Does each concept describe a group of things, events, etc.?

Do other people refer to this group of things in the same way you do, with the same name or label for them?

Does the "concept" have a definition or defining attributes?

Check your lesson objectives/sub-objectives and lesson map from part 1. Are you really teaching concepts? If you do not want students to identify cases or examples, you may be teaching rule using, or verbal information outcomes. These outcomes are described in chapters 3 and 4.

Concept Learning

A person has learned a concept when he or she can apply it. Concept learning is not measured by someone's ability to recall the definition or defining attributes of a concept, although learning a definition may aid in learning the concept. Rather, understanding concepts is determined by the learner's ability to correctly classify new instances of the concept as members of that class, and to discriminate these correct instances from incorrect instances (non-examples) of the concept. For example, a student who can state the defining attributes of deciduous trees has not indicated that he has mastered the concept "deciduous" tree. Instead, the student must be able to identify deciduous trees, when shown both examples of deciduous trees, and non-examples such as evergreen trees or gynkos.

Lesson Components for Concept Learning

Overview

At the minimum, all concept lessons should contain these lesson components:

the objective of the lesson,

a concept definition or statement of defining attributes,

examples of the concept,

explanations of why the examples are examples, i.e., how they possess the defining attributes of the concept,

similar but incorrect instances of the concept (non-examples),

explanations of why the non-examples are non-examples,

practice items that require the student to classify examples of the concept from examples and non-examples,

feedback information presented to the learner that explains why they were correct or incorrect in their practice, and

learning strategies that foster concept learning behavior.

Each of these components will be sequenced differently, depending upon whether you are designing a tutorial or simulation lesson, and whether you choose a deductive or inductive teaching strategy. In some cases, you may prevent the definition first, followed by examples (deductive tutorial). In other cases you may present examples first and have the student try to derive the definitions from them (inductive tutorial). For some concepts, the examples and definitions will be verbal; for other concepts, they will be graphic or graphic and verbal. You may choose to have some of these activities done outside of the computer, by teacher or students.

In this section, we describe how to identify these important lesson components and incorporate them into your lesson. In the lesson design process, each of these components needs to be described before you write the computer lesson. Once you have identified these components you need to select a lesson strategy, whether you want to develop a game, a tutorial, a simulation, a problem solving tool, or some combination. The next section of this chapter will help you select the lesson strategy. Having decided on your strategy, you can then use the final section to design the lesson that embodies that strategy.

In the upcoming sections of this chapter, each lesson component is explained and exemplified. Since each component will comprise one or more computer screens in an actual lesson, we show examples as they would appear on the computer. We begin by designing the lesson objectives.

Concept Objectives

Why Do It: The Effectiveness
of CAI Lesson Objectives

If you have not prepared a statement of the lesson objective in your Readiness unit in part 1, you should prepare one as part of the beginning of the concept learning lesson. Learning research has indicated that students who know the objective of a lesson organize what they learn toward that objective, and achieve that objective more often than students who learn without knowing the objective.

How to Do It: Designing Outcome-
Specific Objectives

The key to writing a successful lesson objective is to be as accurate as possible in the description. The objective should *not* be a statement of content ("this lesson is about nouns"). The objective should describe what the student will learn to do from the lesson, as determined by the learning outcome described in the first section of the workbook.

In this lesson you will learn
how to identify the nouns
in a sentence.

By completing this
counseling lesson you will
learn to identify types
of reinforcement methods.

Each of these examples explains the learned behavior the student is to master upon completion of the lesson. Notice that these outcomes are not verbal information outcomes, because they ask the student to do more than state or recite information. They are not rule using outcomes, because they do not require application of a rule to generate a solution.

You Do It: Write a Concept
Learning Objective

Using the learning analysis you completed in part 1, write out an objective for each one of the concepts.

Objective_____

(Optional Activity) Tell the student the sub-objectives of the lesson, which are the means to the end of the major objective. These sub-objectives are the sub-outcomes you formulated in your lesson map.

Sub-objectives

1. _____

2. _____

3. _____

Check Your Objective(s)

Does your objective tell the learners that they will learn to classify or identify examples of a concept?

Does your objective state the subject matter or context in which these examples will be presented?

Is each sub-objective some skill and knowledge that must be learned to master the objective?

Concept Definitions and Defining Attributes

Why Do It: Definitions as a Source of Concept Learning

A concise and clear statement about the defining characteristics of a concept, coupled with a good example, is an important concept lesson component. Frequently, the definition and examples are presented at the outset of the lesson, as in deductive tutorials. In other cases, the definition is presented later, as in an inductive tutorial. A definition and an example give the student two sources of learning about the concept, enhancing concept understanding and retention.

How to Do It: Presenting Information and Learning Guidance

One of three formats is used to state the defining characteristics of a concept:

State the general class that the concept belongs to, and the characteristic(s) that distinguish it from other concepts in that general class:

A triangle is a **plane figure** with three sides.	Educational Psychology is a **branch of psychology** that examines human learning.

"Plane figure" and "branch of psychology" are general characteristics. "Three sides" and "human learning" are more specific ones.

List the defining characteristics of the concept that make it identifiable:

```
    A triangle:

        has three sides

        has three angles

        is an enclosed figure
```

```
    Positive reinforcement:

        strengthens behavior

        administers preferred stimuli
```

The attributes should be formatted to make them separate the distinct.
Combine the two defining methods into one overall definition:

```
    Positive reinforcement is a
    behaviorist method used to
    modify a subject's behavior.

    This method involves:

        1. strengthening a behavior
        2. administering a desired stimulus
```

The definition format should be used when the concept would have both a general and a specific defining characteristic. The defining attributes format is used when the defining characteristics are all at the same level of generality or specificity. The mixed format is best when there are a general characteristic and several specific ones. Regardless of format, you should try to make your definition as concise as possible.

You Do It: Compose a Concept Definition

To prepare a definition for each new concept, use the following steps:

1. Determine the defining characteristics or attributes that determine membership in the concept class.

2. Write down a rough definition of the concept, listing the essential defining information for the concept(s).

3. Edit the definition (if necessary) down to the two or three most important defining attributes, with an overall length of no more than 25 words, if possible.

4. Choose one of the definition formats described above, and rewrite the definition into that final form. Choose wording suitable to the vocabulary level of the student.

For each new concept to be defined in the lesson, write down a definition in your chosen wording and format:

Concept Definition 1: _____

Concept Definition 2: _____

Self-Check on Definitions

Have all essential attributes been included in each concept?

Is the definition concise?

Does it suit the vocabulary level of your students?

If the definition seems complete and understandable, you can now design concept examples and non-examples for the lesson.

Examples and Non-examples of the Concept

Why Do It: Examples Clarify Concept Attributes

When a concept definition is given, a concept example should also be given with the definition. This is essential for any type of concept instruction. The example helps to clarify the definition, and give the student a prototype to compare to future concept examples. Most studies in concept learning research indicate that young adult and adult learners learn concepts best when they are given both definitions and examples.

How to Do It: Selecting and Sequencing Examples

Any example given with a definition should be the "best" example possible for the student. The "best" example is one that is the most prototypical of that concept; one that would be the most familiar and understandable to the students. If you could use only one example to teach your concept, what would it be? The best example to use first is the one that would be chosen if only one could be used. As the lesson proceeds, more difficult examples can be shown to the student or given as practice, but it is best to start with a simple, easy example. For teenagers, a prototypical example of positive reinforcement would be parents rewarding children for doing chores. For schoolteachers it would be praise given to children for completing assignments.

Generally, the concept definition and best example are presented together, followed by another new concept and its best example:

> <u>Solidification</u>: A change of state in matter where a liquid is changed into a solid.
>
>   (Graphic of ice tray)
>
> A tray of water is frozen until it becomes ice.

An alternate method is to present *all* the concept definitions together, followed by a best example of each concept.

You Do It: Compose a Prototypical Example

For each of the concepts defined in the lesson, create a prototypical example of that concept to clarify the definition. Where a definition and example will both fit onto the computer screen (around 40 words or less), write the definition and example together as they will appear on the computer screen.

Screen Sequence 1 (best examples):

Screen Sequence 2 (definition with examples):

Self-Check on Examples

Is each prototypical example one that would be familiar to students?

Does each example contain all of the defining attributes mentioned in your definition? If not, can you explain why to students?

Additional Examples and Non-examples

*Why Do It: Additional Examples for
Further Clarification*

After an initial example and definition of the concept have been given to the student, another example and/or non-example is useful to help clarify the concept's defining attributes. Another example helps to indicate what the critical defining characteristics are, while a non-example helps to indicate what are *not* critical attributes.

How to Do It: Composing Examples
for Learning Guidance

The new example given to the student should still be a relatively easy and familiar one, yet it should also be different from the first, prototypical example. Often, it is useful to include a short explanation of *why* this example is an example of the concept:

```
Concept: Positive Reinforcement

    Example: A husband hugs his wife
    for fixing the car.

            (GRAPHIC)

    This is an example of positive rein-
    forcement because a preferred state of
    affairs (the hug) is administered to
    strengthen the subject's behavior
    (fixing the car).
```

In the above example, the explanation after the example serves to indicate the critical defining attributes of positive reinforcement that were present in the example.

Non-examples are effective concept learning devices, particularly when the non-examples could be easily confused with the example. Whenever a non-example is used, some explanation should be given of why it is not a correct example. With non-examples, the instructor explains why the non-example does not fit the concept:

```
Concept: Positive Reinforcement

(A similar but incorrect example)

        (GRAPHIC)

Since he has washed the dishes, a wife
tells her husband that he does not have
to take out the garbage.

Note that the subject has performed the
desired behavior, but the behavior is
reinforced by removing an unpleasant
stimulus (taking out the garbage), not
by administering a pleasant stimulus.
```

If you are planning to teach several related concepts in your lesson, each concept example is also a non-example of the other concepts, so you do not have to worry about composing non-examples. For example, if you were teaching the concepts of urban and rural environments, every example of an urban environment is a non-example of a rural environment.

As an option, you can use the non-example explanation to indicate that the non-example is also a correct example of *another* concept that you propose to teach:

> Positive Reinforcement: An Incorrect
> Example
>
> Since he has washed the dishes, a wife
> tells her husband that he does not have
> to take out the garbage.
>
> (GRAPHIC)
>
> Note that the subject has performed the
> desired behavior, but the behavior is
> reinforced by removing an unpleasant
> stimulus (taking out the garbage), not by
> administering a pleasant stimulus. This
> is an example of negative reinforcement.

Note that the correct name for the non-example is added to the end of the explanation.

*You Do It: Compose Examples
and Non-examples*

1. Review the prototypical examples you used with each concept definition, and think of at least one more example that would be familiar to the student, but not as prototypical. Keep examples relatively brief, if possible.

2. Decide if you want to explain why the example is a correct example of the concept; i.e., indicating the defining characteristics of the concept.

3. Determine if there are any relevant non-examples that you want to include in the lesson, and how you will indicate why they are not correct examples of the concept.

4. Determine the sequence of the presentation of the examples/non-examples in the CAI lesson, which example will be presented first, followed by which example or non-example. HINT: if you are going to use non-examples, they should follow the presentation of a correct example of that concept.

5. For each of the concepts in your lesson, write out the concept example/non-example and its explanation, in sequence, as it will appear to the student on the computer screen. Usually, only one concept example/non-example and its explanation will fit on the screen at one time, and at most two. Try to keep the "screen" from becoming too wordy (we discuss screen design in part 3).

Screen Sequence 1 (examples in easy-hard sequence, with explanations):

Screen Sequence 2 (non-examples that match examples, with explanations):

Self-Check on Examples and Non-examples

Is your first example the one you would first present in a classroom lesson?

Have you included a follow-up example that is a little less prototypical than your first example, but not too difficult?

Do your non-examples follow an example of the concept?

Have you indicated why a non-example is not an example, what defining attributes it is missing?

Once students have been given some examples/non-examples, the next step is to have them begin to practice using the concept. This involves providing practice and feedback to the learner.

Practice and Feedback for Concept Learning

Why Do It: Instructional Effects of Practice/Feedback

At this point, you are faced with the decision whether to present additional concept examples/non-examples for the student to study, or to let the student begin to practice identifying examples and non-examples of the concept(s) taught. There are no hard and fast rules on which strategy to use, but several examples are usually sufficient for students to get the general idea of the concept, which is clarified through student practice in identifying examples and receiving feedback.

If you feel the student needs to be shown more examples and non-examples of each concept, simply repeat the *You Do It* activity in the preceding section. It may also be useful to pretest the student as a readiness activity, and use the pretest score to determine how many examples of each concept to present to the learner (see part 3 for a discussion of this technique). Keep in mind, however, that instruction is most effective when the student is *interacting* with the computer, and the student must practice identifying concept examples to really learn the concepts. Through practice, the student learns how to search examples for defining attributes; how to actively apply the concept knowledge gained through the definitions and examples in the lesson.

*How to Do It: Eliciting Student
Performance with Feedback*

Designing practice frames. When teaching more than one concept, the best way to present concept *practice* is to give the student an example and ask the student to choose the concept label that best fits the example:

```
Suzanne has been gradually withdrawing
the food treats that she gives to her dog
when he sits up.

The above is an example of:

a. positive reinforcement
b. negative reinforcement
c. fading
d. shaping
```

When students have a number of concept labels to choose from, the chances of guessing the correct answer are limited. Therefore, it helps to teach related concepts as a set, with practice on the entire set. As an alternative to choosing an answer, have students type in the name of the concept.

Practice exercises should be arranged in an easy-to-hard sequence. The first practice exercise should be one that you feel most students will get right, followed by slightly harder ones, and on to the most difficult. If possible, several examples for each concept taught should be used in the exercise. For example, if three concepts are taught, at least six examples should be used in the lesson, with the more difficult-to-identify examples near the end of the practice sequence.

Whenever possible, true-false and other two-choice questions should be avoided, since the student has a 50-50 chance of guessing the correct answer and thus loses the chance to get corrective feedback for his or her mistakes.

When teaching only one or two concepts, there may be only one or two answer options for the student. In that case, be sure to use a larger series of practice exercises, using both true and false examples of the concept, to increase the probability that lucky guessers will guess an example wrong and receive corrective feedback. Four or five practice examples for one concept would not be out of order. Base the number of practice items needed on the pretest score. The lower the score, the more student practice is required.

Designing feedback frames. Feedback is one of the most important strategies for instruction. Feedback is the response you give to the student for their right or wrong answers to the exercises provided. It is the best way to tell students how they are doing in the lesson, and what they are doing right or wrong. In particular, different kinds of feedback can be provided for different kinds of wrong answers. The use of different types of feedback for different types of responses capitalizes on the answer judging capabilities of the computer, and ensures that the program is more than a simple drill and practice exercise that could just as well be put on paper.

In providing feedback for practice exercises, do not forget that it should be provided for both right and wrong answers. For right answers, the feedback can be a simple "that's right," "good job," or "right! let's try another one," but it can also be more informative. It is possible to use the feedback message on the computer to reinforce the student's knowledge about the concept:

```
Correct! This is a case of positive

reinforcement because the preferred

stimulus (food treat) is administered

after the desired behavior (dog sits up).
```

Instructive feedback for correct answers also means that lucky guessers still receive some instruction about the concept, instead of simply receiving a "correct" message for a guess.

Correct answer feedback is important, but one of the most important parts of any computer lesson is the feedback given for incorrect answers. The best microcomputer instruction has feedback that is tailor-made to the different *kinds* of wrong answers given. In concept learning exercises, the wrong-answer feedback should vary depending on which concept label was incorrectly chosen.

The feedback for an incorrect answer should explain why the concept chosen for the example was incorrect. In other words, the feedback should mention which of the incorrect concept's defining attributes were *not* present in the example. It also helps to present the exercise example along with the feedback, so that students can look at the example and the explanation together.

```
Since he has washed the dishes,
a wife tells her husband that he
does not have to take out the garbage.

             (GRAPHIC)

No, this is not a case of punishment.
Punishment involves administering some
unpleasant state of affairs. Here an
unpleasant state of affairs is avoided.
```

Notice that the feedback in the above example does not give students the correct answer. This is because you may want them to try the example again before you give them the answer. This strategy can be used only when students initially have three or more possible choices for the answer, since repeating the question means that one choice is automatically eliminated (the one already chosen incorrectly).

If students will not get another chance at the exercise, then the correct answer can be given to them. However, the answer should follow an explanation of why the student choice was incorrect. Also, both the correct choice and an explanation of why it was correct can be included:

```
Feedback with Correct-Choice Explanation

No, this is not a case of punishment.
Punishment involves administering some
unpleasant state of affairs. Here this
state of affairs is avoided, which makes
it a case of negative reinforcement.
```

Once you have given the student the answer, you should move on to another practice item. However, you should have the computer programmed to repeat practice items that students have missed. Students can be given the missed item again immediately after they have missed it. As an alternative, the missed item can be presented later on in the practice program, after students have practiced on other examples. If you give the student the answer, the practice item should be repeated later on in the program.

You Do It: Compose Practice and
Feedback Frames

To compose the concept learning exercise:

1. Write out a relatively easy example for each concept.

2. Write out a more difficult example for each concept.

3. (Optional) Write out some more difficult examples for each concept. You do not have to write one for every concept if you have a large set of related concepts.

4. Review and edit the examples. Keep in mind that the example must fit on the screen along with the answer options and screen directions.

5. Number the examples in the sequence in which they will appear on the screen.

To compose the feedback for the exercise:

1. Decide if you want the students to have a second or third chance at the quesiton if they get it wrong.

2. Taking each example in turn, write down the feedback message that you will give to students:
    a. If they get the answer right.
    b. If they incorrectly choose answer x, If they incorrectly choose answer y, etc.
    c. If they make an unexpected reply, like hitting key "z," or RETURN.
    d. (Optional) if they got the answer right on their second or third try.

3. Decide if you want the computer program to repeat practice items that students missed on the first or second try.

4. Decide if you want the repeats to occur immediately after they have missed the item, or after other practice items.

When composing the feedback, consider putting the feedback on the screen with the practice question, if space permits.

Compose a complete concept learning exercise for the concepts of your lesson, using the directions above. Write each question and feedback response separately, just as the student would see it on the screen. Write each question and feedback frame on a separate sheet of paper, and identify each sheet as an exercise or feedback frame. You should number the question frames so that you do not mix up the sequence when you are programming the computer. It also helps to note the correct answer to the question. Since you will have different types of feedback for each question, depending on the student response, you will have more than one feedback frame for each question.

Each feedback frame should have some label written on the back or bottom of the paper, such as, "1st wrong answer feedback for question 3," or "correct second try, question 1."

Screen Sequence 1 (1st practice question frames):

Screen Sequence 2 (feedback frames for 1st questions):

Screen Sequence 3 (2nd set of practice questions):

Screen Sequence 4 (feedback frames for 2nd set):

Self-Check on Practice and Feedback

Have you included enough practice items for all the students?

Do they have opportunities to try multiple-option answers again?

Have you anticipated all possible right and wrong answers? Have you prepared for unanticipated answers?

Does your wrong answer feedback vary with the type of concept practice error made? Does it tell students which attributes they missed or mixed up?

Does your feedback teach students as well as inform them that they are right or wrong?

Once you have finished designing the practice and feedback components of the lesson, you have walked through all of the general instructional components of a computer lesson for concepts. The next step is to modify these to suit the particular learning strategies that you will use on the computer.

Learning Strategies for Concept Learning

Why Do It: Facilitating Concept Acquisition

Concept learning, like most types of learning, does not come naturally. It is an acquired skill, or rather a set of acquired skills. As we pointed out in part 1, concept learning can require learning sub-outcomes, such as verbal information. These sub-outcomes enable us to learn concepts.

One such required skill is a learning strategy skill. Learning strategies help students learn how to learn. Concept learning strategies teach students to learn how to learn concepts. Without a learning strategy, students often try to learn such concepts by verbal learning techniques, such as memorizing a definition. However, concept learning requires deeper processing of information than is required for memorization or verbal learning. In order to learn concepts, students must access prior knowledge and relate the new concepts attributes to something that they *already* know, as indicated in chapter 2.

Learning strategies are different from the learning guidance techniques discussed in this chapter in "Additional Examples and Non-examples." Learning guidance is designed to help the learner accomplish the objective, that is, to identify examples of a specific concept. Learning strategies, on the other hand, help the learner to learn concepts in general, that is, to acquire concept learning skills. Learning strategies provide the learner with generalizable learning skills that can be used to learn other concepts. They work because they are generative. Generative activities require learners to think in more meaningful ways about concepts, to relate the concept to prior learning. They generate meaning for it.

How to Do It: Embedding Concept
Learning Strategies in CAI

There are many learning strategies that facilitate concept learning. Here we present three strategies that have been effective in helping learners acquire concepts: an exemplifying strategy, a paraphrasing strategy, and a worksheet strategy.

Exemplifying strategy. The exemplifying strategy requires learners to think of and list examples of the concept being learned. As indicated in the lesson components section, a CAI lesson presents matched examples/ non-examples or prototypical examples, and indicates the presence of attributes in the examples.

If learners successfully integrate the definition and examples to learn the concept, then they should be able to generate their own examples. By thinking of their own concept examples, learners reason beyond the definition and example given.

After providing examples and practice in your CAI lesson, have the learner generate a concept example:

```
From your own experience, can you
think of an instance where
positive reinforcement was used?
Type in your example on the next line.


_____.
```

Repeat this activity at least once. If the concept is difficult or the students are having trouble, have them generate three or four examples. Be careful. Some concepts do not have many examples, so do not frustrate the students by having them generate more examples than you could yourself!

Paraphrasing strategy. Another very simple strategy to implement in CAI is paraphrasing. Near the end of the concept lesson, simply ask learners to paraphrase or "tell in their own words" what the concept means. No clues, definitions, or descriptions should be available to students.

Paraphrasing forces learners to relate the concept to their prior knowledge and describe it in a way that makes sense to them:

```
        In your own words, what does

        positive reinforcement mean

        to you?
        _____
```

An alternative to this paraphrasing strategy is "teach it to your little brother." Ask learners to describe how they would explain this concept to their seven-year-old brother. This forces students to search for the simplest, most comprehensible way of explaining the concept.

Definition worksheet. We have said that generative learning requires that the learner relate the new concept to what she or he already knows and to related ideas. The definition worksheet forces students to relate the new concept to what they already know, to compare the concept to other related ideas. The worksheet requires learners to identify several relationships for each concept: characteristics or descriptors, opposites, similarities, antecedents, evidence, subsets, and supersets. It is particularly useful when learners have to learn *sets* of related concepts.

To use a worksheet, introduce the worksheet at the beginning of the lesson. As concept information is encountered in the lesson, learners go to the worksheet by pressing a definition key (D option on the keyboard). The worksheet would show up on the computer screen and students could fill in the information:

```
Concept: Isosceles Triangle

Type the number you want to fill in:

1. Characteristics of (what makes this
   a _____)
2. Broader term (this concept is a kind
   or part of)
3. Narrower term (part, kind, or type of)
4. Similar term or idea
5. Opposite term or idea
```

Not every type of relationship needs to be listed for each concept. Use only those relationships for which there is an obvious instance to fill in. To make this strategy most effective, have the computer print out the worksheet in a table format, with the concepts taught in one column and each of the types of relationships in another column. This will help students make comparisons and contrasts between concepts. As part of concept practice, students can compare different concepts in terms of certain relationships. The more interrelating they do, the better they discriminate between concepts.

You Do It: Construct a Concept
Learning Strategy

Select a strategy or set of strategies that you think will help your students actively process the concept definitions and examples. Reviewing your concept definitions and examples, incorporate learning strategies into your concept program. This can be done by rewriting some of the concept frames, or by adding additional frames.

Screen Sequence 1 (learning strategy frames for definitions/examples):

Self-Check on Strategies

Have you included a learning strategy for each concept?

Does your strategy require the student to actively process the information by writing, creating, and thinking about the concept?

Selecting a Lesson Strategy

Why Do It: The Variety of Lesson Strategies

As we indicated at the beginning of this chapter, certain instructional components are vital to any concept learning lesson, components such as definitions, examples, and practice/feedback instruction. However, the particular teaching strategy that you select to deliver these components can vary. The tutorial method of presenting definitions followed by examples and practice/feedback segments is an extremely popular method. However, there are other strategies that can be used, strategies such as simulations, games, or drill and practice routines.

Simulations, games, problem solving tools, and drill and practice routines are all "non-instructional." That is, they all presuppose that the student has to some degree already learned the content, or is learning it from some other source. Thus, a concept simulation may be used after a student has learned concepts in class, or through a deductive tutorial. These strategies can be used to enhance students' prior concept knowledge. They can also be used in conjunction with teaching strategies such as inductive or deductive tutorials.

In this section, we provide a short, step-by-step guide to selecting the type of lesson strategy that best suits your needs.

**You Do It: Select a
Lesson Strategy**

To select the proper lesson strategy, a decision making aid is outlined below. Answer the aid's questions in order, and then follow the directions given:

Step 1. Does the major lesson objective require learning a concept?

If yes, go to step 3.

If no, go to step 2.

Step 2. Does one of the lesson sub-objectives require concept learning?

If yes, go to step 3.

If no, go to another chapter. You do not need a concept lesson. Review chapter 1.

Step 3. Have students already learned the concepts of the learning objectives, and are they ready to try classifying examples?

If they are ready to classify examples, go to step 4.

If they must first learn the concepts, go to step 6.

Step 4. Do you want to provide basic practice on concept identification, or do you want the learners to transfer the concepts to real life scenarios?

For review/practice, go to step 5.

For transfer, go to step 9.

Step 5. You need to develop a drill/game for this lesson. Go to the drill and practice part of this chapter to develop a drill/game. Also, see step 10.

Step 6. Will the student need to apply the concept to a wide variety of settings (e.g., school, home, work, etc.)?

If wide application, go to step 7.

If more specific application, go to step 8.

Step 7. You need to construct a tutorial, and an inductive tutorial may be your best bet. Go to the tutorial part of the next section. Also, go to step 10 below.

Step 8. You need to construct a tutorial lesson, probably a deductive one. Go to the tutorial part of the next section. Also, see step 10 below.

Step 9. You need to develop a simulation. Go to the simulations part of the next section. Also, see step 10.

Step 10. Will you need to construct on-screen problem solving aids for the student, to help them learn how to use concepts?

If yes, see "Problem Solving Tools for Concept Learning" after you have reviewed the tutorial/game/drill/simulation section you selected.

If no, go to the teaching strategy you selected in the previous step.

This aid is meant to help you select a strategy, but it should not be regarded as law. Once you have previewed a strategy recommended by the aid, you may want to review other strategies and choose one of those instead. For example, you may not want to use an inductive tutorial, and choose a deductive tutorial instead. In particular, some of these strategies may be used together. Almost any tutorial can have one of the other strategies piggy-backed onto it, to enhance concept learning.

CAI Lesson Strategies

Tutorials

Why Do It: Tutorials as Primary Learning Strategies

The primary method for teaching concepts is the tutorial. The tutorial method is especially important when the student has to learn the concept definitions and attributes before attempting any concept classification exercises. Tutorials are ways of teaching the students what they *must* learn. Games, simulations, and drills are ways of exercising and refining what they have *already* learned.

There are two types of tutorials: inductive and deductive. A deductive tutorial presents the definitions and examples to the student, followed by student practice. An inductive tutorial presents examples and non-examples to the students and has them derive (induce) the correct definition and label for the concept, followed by student practice. The deductive method is easier to design, and more likely to produce quick learning. An effective inductive lesson may be remembered better, and the concepts learned may be better transferred to new situations the learner encounters.

How to Do It: Constructing a Deductive Tutorial

Deductive tutorials can best be constructed by following the steps outlined in the lesson components section of this chapter. For concept tutorials, deductive tutorials involve:

1. Presenting the concept objective.
2. Presenting a definition or defining attributes.
3. Presenting examples and non-examples of the concept, starting with a prototypical example.
4. Presenting practice to the student in an easy-to-hard sequence with branching.
5. Presenting feedback for correct and incorrect examples.

The practice and feedback sections can also incorporate elements of games, simulations, or drills, depending upon the instructor's preference. For example, students can use a tutorial to learn about the concepts of evaporation and dehydration, and then play a game on this topic later on. These other strategies are outlined later in this chapter.

You Do It: Construct a Deductive Tutorial

Follow the steps of the lesson components section of this chapter:

Present concept objective(s)

Present definition/defining attributes

Present examples and non-examples

Present sequenced practice

Provide differential feedback for answers

Complete each of the *You Do It* parts of the lesson components section and you will have completed most of the essential components of a deductive tutorial.

*How to Do It: Constructing
an Inductive Tutorial*

To construct an inductive concept learning lesson, present the concept examples at the beginning of the lesson and have the student generate the definition from the examples given. To do this, the lesson usually will pose questions to students about each example they see, using a series of questions to help the student induce the definition. Most inductive lessons follow the design sequence outlined below.

Present the lesson objective. Explain what students will do in the inductive lesson:

```
             Principles of Conditioning
                    Lesson One


    In this lesson you will be given
    some examples of conditioning activities.
    You will be asked to figure out what
    kinds of conditioning are being used.
```

Present directions to the student on how to answer the questions and examples given in the lesson. This should include an explanation of why you want them to induce the definitions.

```
    You will be given examples of one of
    four conditioning techniques. You will
    have to figure out what technique is
    used in each example.

    We could tell you what technique is used
    in each example, but if you figure them
    out yourself you will remember them
    better.
```

Present examples and non-examples of each concept, in the general order described in the lesson components section. However the lesson must require that learners figure out the critical attributes of the concept, instead of being told:

```
Every time his dog sits up
properly, a boy gives her
a bone.

        (GRAPHIC)

Is the boy trying to
strengthen or weaken
the dog's behavior?
```

Learners will then induce the definition of the concept.

Provide explanatory feedback for each of the student's attempts, whether the answer is right or wrong:

```
            Right!!

In this case the boy wants the
dog to continue sitting up, so
he wants to strengthen her
behavior.

This is an example of positive
reinforcement.
```

After the student induces the attributes of a concept, ask him or her to identify a prototypical example of the concept, or an easy non-example:

```
Every time a pigeon pecks at a
red button, it is given corn.

      (GRAPHIC)

Is this an example of
positive reinforcement?
```

```
When a dog barks, his
owner takes his food away.

      (GRAPHIC)

Is this an example of
positive reinforcement?
```

As an option, have students generate their own examples of the concept in question, as an off-screen activity (see the learning strategies section). A student or teacher can evaluate the examples.

Introduce the next concept. If the next concept is similar to the previous concept, ask the student to induce the difference:

```
When his dog sits up, a
boy removes his flea collar.

This is not a case of
positive reinforcement.
How is it different?
```

Present an example of this new concept, and repeat the steps above. When this cycle is complete for all concepts in the lesson, introduce more difficult examples for the students to practice classifying, according to the lesson components guidelines.

In some cases, deductive and inductive procedures can be mixed in the same tutorial. For example, have the student induce the *basic* definition of a concept; then provide further explanation of the definition to them. You can also *explain* difficult concept examples, instead of asking the student to induce their characteristics.

You Do It: Compose an Inductive Tutorial

Beginning with a screen that describes the objective of the lesson, construct a draft of an inductive concept learning lesson. Take each lesson concept in turn, make a prototypical example of each, and construct a series of questions about the defining attributes of each concept. Be sure to include feedback frames for right or wrong answers.

Screen Sequence 1 (objective, purpose, directions):

Screen Sequence 2 (examples with questions about defining attributes for students to induce):

Screen Sequence 3 (feedback for student inductions):

Screen Sequence 4 (examples where the student must classify an example):

Screen Sequence 5 (feedback for classification):

Drill and Practice Routines

Why Do It: Drill and Practice for
Learning Improvement

Drill and practice routines are one of the most frequently used strategies for computer instruction. A drill and practice routine administers a problem exercise to the student, takes the student's response to the problem, judges it as correct or incorrect, (usually) provides feedback, and administers a new problem or repeats the same one. It can also keep track of the number of times a student missed a particular question, and the total number of correct and incorrect answers. Drill and practice routines are designed for students who have already learned a given learning outcome: their purpose is to test or refine the student's knowledge.

While drill and practice routines appear simple to construct, good routines can use a number of subtle techniques. A good drill and practice routine for concept learning should employ most or all of the following features:

A description of the objectives, benefits, and purpose of the lesson.

Practice that requires identification/classification of examples.

Practice examples of a wide range of difficulty, where the concept examples become increasingly difficult and/or students choose a level of difficulty.

Feedback to students about the answers they missed, and what defining attributes they missed or confused.

Review of practice items, where an item missed is repeated right after it is missed or later on in the drill.

Student recordkeeping, where the computer lesson will record and report student performance.

How to Do It: Constructing a Drill
and Practice Routine

Give students an overview of the upcoming lesson. Include the lesson objective, purpose, and directions:

```
Drill 1: Reinforcement Methods

This drill will help you learn
to classify applications of four
types of reinforcement.  It will
help you recognize how to use these
methods in real life.
```

```
Directions

For each description
given, type in the
name of the technique.
Try to be careful with
your spelling.
```

Create a set of examples for the drill. These should vary in their difficulty, and should range across all areas of application for the lesson concepts. For example, the concepts of reinforcement can be applied to animal training, classrooms, and business. You can design the lesson to present the examples to all students in an easy-to-hard sequence, beginning with the most prototypical examples. Or, you can have the student select a difficulty range from a menu:

```
Choose a practice level:

   1. easy
   2. more difficult
   3. difficult
```

Note: If you intend to evaluate the student's drill performance as a test, it may be better to give all students the same drill sequence.

Design each example as a "drill frame." The frame should not only contain an example, it should be numbered, so the students can keep track of the items they have completed:

```
Item: 6   Behavioral Methods

   If a teacher praises a student
   for handing in her homework on
   time.

   What principle is the teacher using?
   (type in your answer) _____.
```

The drill items can be multiple choice or open answer questions (as the one above). The open answer questions test the students' memory of the concept name as well as their ability to identify an example. However, open answer questions can be more difficult for the computer to judge.

Design the feedback messages for the drill. Some drills do not give the students any explanation of why they missed an answer, it just tells them that they were wrong. For concept drills, it is a good idea to explain the defining attributes the student missed or confused:

```
      Your answer was:

   negative reinforcement

   Incorrect. In this case,
   a preferred stimulus was
   administered to the student.
```

Note that the correct answer was not given to the student, just a cue about the nature of the correct answer (and the mistake). Instead of giving the students the answer, have them try again, particularly if this is their first miss on the item.

Select a branching strategy for the drill. If students miss an item, do one of the three things: (a) send them back to try again, (b) give them the answer and present a new item, (c) have them try the item again later in the drill, after 3-6 other items. All of these are viable branching strategies. However, if the student has more than two choices left, it is best to have him or her try the item again, now or later:

```
Your answer:

    negative reinforcement

In this example, a positive
stimulus is administered.
It is not an aversive stimulus.

Try this one again.
```

```
Your answer:

    negative reinforcement

In this example, positive
stimulus is administered.
It is not an aversive stimulus.

    Later, we'll try this one again.
```

You can also arrange special branches for students who are doing well in the drill. If students have gotten a number of drill items right on the first try, they can skip some of the easier concept examples, and go directly to harder ones.

As a close to the drill, you should give the student some feedback about his or her overall performance. If the student was not exposed to all of the practice items, you can have him or her do it again:

```
Drill 1    Reinforcement Methods

        Final Score

You identified 60% on the 1st try
               30% on the 2nd try

    Would you like to try again?
```

You can also have the lesson coded to store each student's performance record, so that you can examine it later.

You Do It: Construct a Concept Drill

Beginning with the introductory drill screens, outline a drill and practice routine on paper. Construct all practice items first. Next, develop a branching plan for each practice item, such as how often students will repeat missed items, and when they will repeat them. Finally, develop the feedback and branching messages. The same screen can contain feedback and information about where the student will be branched.

Screen Sequence 1 (objectives, purpose, directions, title, menu):

Screen Sequence 2 (drill examples that vary in difficulty and context, with multiple examples for each concept):

Screen Sequence 3 (feedback and branching messages to student, with feedback tailored to type of concept attributes missed/confused):

Screen Sequence 4 (scores and summary feedback):

Games

Why Do It: Games as Motivating Practice

Computer games are an established part of our society's recreations and diversions. Both adults and children find computer games to be challenging and interesting. For instruction, computer games can challenge students to perform the desired learning outcomes in a competitive environment. The elements of challenge and competition make games a motivational tool for students to practice and refine skills they have already learned.

To be a game, the strategy must have a criterion for achievement or winning. Games incorporate elements of competition or challenge. They also contain rules for playing the game. Where simulations incorporate elements of real life situations, a game can be a fantasy or fiction scenario. When a game has real life elements to its scenarios, it is called a *simulation game*.

For concept learning, games can be used as a substitute for standard drill and practice routines. The game can be incorporated as part of a tutorial lesson, or it can be used as a separate practice module. Either way, the game should require example classification from the player(s). The game can include scorekeeping, degrees of difficulty, and awards for achievement.

How to Do It: Constructing a
Concept Game

Present the purpose, rules, and directions of the game:

```
            Conditioning Capers

In this game you will see examples
of different kinds of conditioning.
You need to decide what type of
conditioning is exemplified, and
choose the letter that corresponds
to the correct answer (a,b,c, or d)

For each correct answer, you will
receive 10 points.
```

Present the concept learning questions/exercises. Be sure that they are randomly presented and that you have a large pool of questions. Some games may have over 100 questions.

```
    Question 1:   Score 0

    (EXAMPLE GRAPHIC)

    What conditioning technique
    is this?

    a. pos. reinf.     b. neg. reinf.

    c. punishment      d. fading
```

Remember that a concept game requires identification or classification behaviors. Otherwise it is not a concept game.

You may want to group the questions into order of difficulty: easy, hard, and difficult. You should award more points to problems that learners prefer not to do, to increase the likelihood that they will do them. This is an excellent and proven incentive to get learners to work harder. By offering a wide range of game examples, you help the student transfer the concept to new situations.

```
Question 8:    Score 90

You're doing great! Choose a question:
1. Easy (10 points)
2. Hard (20 points)
3. Tough (25 points)
(The record is 440 points!!)
```

You may provide only knowledge of results for the students' game choices, not feedback that explains how or why they were wrong. Your decision depends on how instructive or remedial you want to make the lesson. If the game is a practice adjunct to a concept tutorial that had practice and feedback, you may omit feedback. In any case, try to make the knowledge of results bright and attractive.

```
            You're right!!!
               10 pts.

        300 = Master

        200 = Apprentice

        100 = Beginner

    You now have 180 points.
    Let's try another!!!!
```

During the game players should be periodically updated about their scores and performance.

At the end of the game summarize the learner's performance, comparing it to the best performances done at the game, or some level of achievement.

```
TERRIFIC!  (TROPHY GRAPHIC)

You scored 370 points!

This makes you a CONCEPT MASTER!

Your score was only 70 points
off of the all time record!
```

You Do It: Construct a Concept Game

Starting with the objective and directions to the game, construct a concept game for a set of lesson concepts. Build in both the practice and scorekeeping functions of the game:

Screen Sequence 1 (objective purpose and directions):

Screen Sequence 2 (easy-to-hard game examples, with performance updates):

Screen Sequence 3 (game totals, comparisons, awards):

Simulations

Why Do It: Simulations as
Real Life Exercises

One of the most effective ways to promote concept learning is to use simulations for student practice. A simulation is a simulated real life scenario displayed on the computer, which the student has to act upon. A simulation is more than a simple practice exercise, it is a situation of which the student becomes a part, and has to resolve through choice or decision. Depending upon the choice or decision the student makes, the lesson scenario will change.

Simulations are most frequently used to teach problem solving outcomes, since most simulations require complex problem solving behavior. However, basic simulations can be designed that require concept learning via example classification. These simulations are often used as adjuncts to concept tutorials.

How to Do It: Constructing a Concept Simulation

Begin by explaining the objectives and purpose of the simulation:

```
The Behavioral Teacher

Today, you will assume the
role of a classroom teacher.

       (GRAPHIC)

As you encounter different
classroom problems, you will
have to select a reinforcement
strategy and identify it.
```

```
The Elements Master

In this lesson, you will
use temperature and pressure
to alter types of matter.


When you change the state of
a type of matter, you will
have to identify the type of
change you made.
```

Present a problem scenario in which students participate by choosing some course of action. The scenario can be a trip, a business situation, anything interesting and familiar to the student:

```
Welcome to your 3rd grade class at
Concept Elementary

(GRAPHIC)  Prof. (student's name)

       Today, you will be teaching
       Civil War history.
```

```
To begin, choose a
substance to modify:

   a.  water
   b.  steel
   c.  helium
```

The key is to make the scenario a real one; one that students understand and in which the concepts are applied in real life. As in the example above, students can choose their starting points in the simulation.

Depending upon the choice the student makes, the next screen will present a scenario that reacts to the choice made. Different student choices result in different screens. As part of the scenario, the student must engage in concept learning performance by classifying examples/non-examples:

Oh! Oh! John seems to be talking
to Fred, and he won't listen to you!
What will you do to stop him?

(GRAPHIC)

a) take away   c) hit him with
   his lunch   a ruler

b) tell him he   d) be sarcastic
   is acting up

You have a pool of
water at room temp.
How do you want to
change it?

(GRAPHIC)
    Temp. = 70 F

Press H to heat it
Press C to cool it

You have hit John with a ruler.

What reinforcement technique have
you used?

a) pos. reinf.   c) neg. reinf.

b) punishment   d) extinction

You have now changed
the water to ice.

    Temp. = 32 F

What change in
matter have you made?

_____

As with any student practice, feedback must be provided about their choices, as prescribed earlier in this chapter:

Very good Professor Bill!
You were using an aversive
stimulus on John, to eliminate
his behavior.

(GRAPHIC)

Your answer: sublimation

No, you did not change a
liquid to gas/vapor.

Try this one again.
Hint: you made it <u>solid</u>

After feedback has been given, continue the scenario with further decisions and concept identification tasks:

```
John has apologized to you for his
errant behavior. Since he has been
so nice, you decide to:

(GRAPHIC)

a) quit hitting him   b) compliment him

c) give him back      d) "gold star" him
   his lunch
```

```
Now that you have
a block of ice, what
will you do next?

   (GRAPHIC)

Press H to Heat
Press C to Cool
```

Thus, the simulation can continue a scenario that requires concept-based learning performance.

Continue the simulation until all scenario decisions have been made or students have sufficient practice with concept identification.

After a student completes a simulation, many instructors hold a "debriefing" session, where the student discusses the simulation with the teacher and/or other classmates. Some debriefing questions for concept simulations would be:

What did you learn from the simulation?

How could you use these concepts in real life?

What were the toughest choices to make?

There are other useful simulation features that can be combined with your lesson, depending on the content of the concepts taught:

Use a light touch; keep the simulation fun.

If possible, have students choose their roles in the simulation (doctor-nurse, teacher-student).

Use graphics of people, places, and objects, even if they are simple sketches.

Highlight the concept attributes of examples, by underlining or explaining features of the scenario that reflect these attributes.

Use a concept problem solving tool to remind students of the concept attributes.

You Do It: Construct a Simulation

Using the procedures outlined above, rough out a simulation on paper, beginning with the creation of the scenario:

Screen Sequence 1 (title of simulation, directions):

Screen Sequence 2 (scenarios with choices and examples for identification):

Screen Sequence 3 (feedback on choices made in first scenarios):

Screen Sequence 4 (changes in scenarios for each choice made in first scenarios):

Screen Sequence 5 (decisions and identifications for altered scenarios):

Problem Solving Tools for Concept Learning

Why Do It: Problem Solving Tools as
Concept Learning Aids

To begin with, problem solving tools should not be confused with problem solving learning outcomes. Problem solving tools are instructional aids that are used for all types of learning outcomes: rules, concepts, problem solving, even verbal information. These tools are instructional adjuncts to tutorials, games, simulations, and drills.

Problem solving tools are aids that are embedded into the computer program itself. They help the student solve the problem of mastering the lesson outcomes. For example, a problem solving tool for learning the rules of time management can be a checklist of guidelines for using the rules of time management, which can be called onto the screen when the student is trying to apply the rules to a time management problem. Similarly, a computer database can be a problem solving tool that helps store the information the student needs to solve a rule, concept, or problem solving problem.

Problem solving tools are useful because they provide on-screen help to students who need to know how to solve the problem. As with many on-screen aids, the tool can *model* the thought processes or questions that an expert would use.

There are a wide variety of simple and sophisticated problem solving tools for computer lessons. For our purposes, we review one of the most basic and important tools for concept learning instruction: the use of an on-screen learning aid for concept learning problems.

How to Do It: Constructing a
Concept Learning Tool

A concept learning tool should help the student identify concepts. To do this, the aid should focus on asking or telling the student about the critical defining attributes of the concept:

Concept Checklist: Conditioning Concepts

	Pos.	Neg.	Pun.
Strengthen Behavior?	x	x	
Weaken Behavior?			x
Positive stim. adm.?	x		
Negative stim. adm.?			x
Negative stim. avoided?		x	

The aid can also take the form of an expert aid. The aid duplicates the questioning process that an "expert" concept learner would use to identify the concept(s):

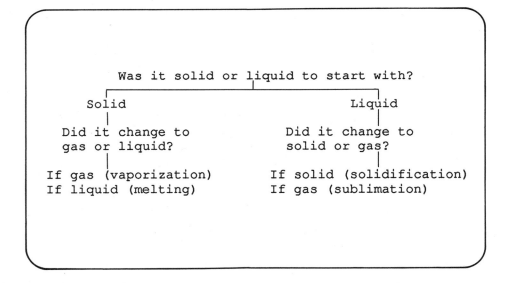

Make the aid available to the student, to be called up during any concept-based practice or exercise in which you will allow the student to receive help. For example, the tool can be available only for the first two or three practice exercises the student does (or in the early stage of a game or simulation):

```
Ann will not let Phil play his radio
until he does his homework.

    The above is a case of _____.

    Enter answer and press RETURN.

                      Press "H" for HELP
```

The "Help" function will call up the problem solving tool. You can also have this help automatically provided to the student, if the student should miss more than two practice items in a row, or miss the same item several times.

The on-screen aid can also provide examples of each concept for the student to review, either with or without any description of critical attributes:

```
Some examples of positive reinforcement:

   A pigeon gets corn for pecking a button.

   A student gets a "gold star" for doing
   her homework.

   A husband gets a hug for taking out the
   garbage.
```

You Do It: Construct a Concept
Problem Solving Tool

Review the lesson's concept attributes and examples, and decide on an aid (or aids) that you think will provide the most help to students when they are classifying concept examples. If possible, organize the aid into a single-screen tool that can be used for all of the concepts of the lesson.

Screen Sequence 1 (aid):

Screen Sequence 2 (other aids):

Using Database Management Tools
to Aid Concept Learning

How to Do It: Using Databases to
Highlight Defining Attributes

In the verbal information chapter, we described the use of database management systems to facilitate the recall of verbal information. We defined databases as organized collections of records which are broken down into fields. These records and fields define the structure of the information. Requiring learners to study such databases, or even create their own, facilitates verbal information learning. In addition, database management systems may be just as effective in facilitating concept learning.

How can such database activities be used for concept learning? They are used to help students learn and discriminate the defining attributes of a set of related concepts, and to recall examples. When students must learn a family of concepts, the concepts can each be treated as a separate record. The defining attributes and other relevant information can be recorded as fields in each concept record. Following are two concept records from a database on figures:

(Field 1)	Concept Name: Triangle	Concept Name: Quadrilateral
(Field 2)	Attributes: 3 sides	Attributes: 3 sides
(Field 3)	Degrees: 180	Degrees: 360
(Field 3)	Irrelevant: Size Shape	Irrelevant: Size Shape
(Field 4)	Forms: Right Triangle Isosceles Triangle	Forms: Square Rectangle

In particular, the database can emphasize what features are important to identify in concept examples and non-examples. It can specify the key defining characteristics, and what seemingly important details are irrelevant. By focusing on the defining and the irrelevant attributes, the database helps a student learn to discriminate between concepts that have overlapping characteristics, such as the concepts of positive and negative reinforcement.

How to Do It: Selecting and Developing a Database Strategy

Determine if a database tool would help your students learn concepts. Look at the concepts that students must learn. Are there more than two related concepts? Do they have defining characteristics that might be confused with each other? If the answer to these two questions is yes, a database might be helpful.

Determine if you want to show students a database or have them construct their own. If you want the database to function as a help or review aid, you probably want to construct one yourself. If you want the database to function as a learning strategy aid or practice exercise, students should construct their own, which forces them to actively organize and relate concept information:

Concept: conditioned response

Description: target behavior
            reinforced

Antecedent: conditioned stimulus

Consequent: reward, reinforcement

Examples: selling effort,
          sitting on command

Complete the following concept:

   Concept: conditioned response

   Description: _____

   Antecedent: _____

   Consequent: _____

   Examples: _____

The first example shows a database, the second is constructive. In any given lesson, both database strategies can be used. Students can be given the database at different times, and then construct their own.

Decide how to use the database in the lesson. If students are to be shown the database, it can be used as a help or review segment of the concept lesson. If they are to construct one, it can be used as a practice exercise at different points in the lesson, or as a final test or practice:

The next reinforcement concept
we will discuss is shaping.

Press "R" to review concepts.

Press RETURN to go on.

The next reinforcement concept
we will discuss is shaping.

Before we do, let's see if you
can describe the concepts you
have learned.

   RETURN to make a database.

In the first example, students will study a given database as needed. In the second, they will construct one. Either strategy can help students improve their ability to classify examples and non-examples.

Determine the key elements of the concept database. Obviously, defining attributes are key items of information. However, confusing or deceptive "non-attributes" may be just as important (i.e., reinforcers do not have to be physical things). Prototypical examples and deceptive non-examples can be a useful part of the database, whether the database is given by the teacher or constructed by students.

```
Concept: positive reinforcement

Attributes: response strengthened
            preferred stimulus
               administered

Non-attributes: response weakened
                aversive stimulus removed

Examples: pigeon gets corn for pecking
              button
          student gets "gold star" for
              attendance

Non-example: Student avoids lecture by
               attending
```

Defining attributes, non-attributes, examples, and non-examples will all be stored as separate fields in the record of each concept.

If you are using the database as a help or reference tool, it can be programmed for students to browse through specific fields of information across all concepts. For example, students can search "defining attributes" for all concepts in the lesson:

```
To review reinforcement concepts,
select what you would like to see:

1  defining attributes

2  examples and non-examples

3  all data on each concept

Enter number of your choice and RETURN
```

Consider adding some of the following options to the database, to improve its effectiveness:

If you give students a concept database, have them arrange the information in new fields or records, or have them add onto the information. This encourages active processing. Check your database first to make sure that its structure can be rearranged.

If students are making a database, have them complete one single field for each concept record (doing the "attributes" field only), and then complete another field. This strategy makes students compare all the concepts each time they complete a field.

If students are constructing a database, set the computer to record students' input. You can then have their database input printed out for you to evaluate.

You Do It: Construct a Concept Database

If the amount and relationship of lesson concepts is appropriate for a concept database, construct a database tool or have the students construct one:

Screen Sequence 1 (displays of database information given by you:

Screen Sequence 2 (students practice making or using database):

Screen Sequence 3 (screens that tell or guide students to use the database. You can rewrite lesson screens to include a review or help command to see the database, and/or create new screens that announce a database construction exercise for students):

Evaluating CAI Concept Lesson Tutorials

Most of the CAI software created and used by teachers is tutorial in nature, whether they produce it or purchase it. Therefore, we have included a brief section on how to evaluate CAI tutorials. When the final lesson is complete, review the lesson using the checklist outlined below. This checklist can also be used as an evaluation tool for commercially made software.

When evaluating commercial computer software, the first question to ask is "Does the lesson teach concept learning outcomes?" This cannot be judged by a declaration in the program title or documentation that the program teaches concepts: it can only be done by reviewing the program itself, to see if the program actually tries to teach the classification of examples based on definitions or defining attributes. Sometimes, a purported concept lesson will actually teach rule or verbal information learning outcomes.

CHECKLIST

	Not Done		Adequate		Very Good
	0	1	2	3	4

1. Readiness activities provided?

2. Lesson require classification of examples (with non-examples)?

3. Defining attributes are stated or student is required to induce them?

4. Varied examples/non-examples are provided?

5. Examples/non-examples are explained?

6. Practice provided (via drill and practice, simulations, games, etc.)?

7. Correct/incorrect answer feedback?

8. Instructions/directions to students?

Whether you are evaluating your own program or commercial software, it is critical that you have several students try out the program. Sit down next to each student and watch him or her try out the program. Can students follow the directions? Do the concept examples make sense? Can they do the practice exercises? Take notes as you go concerning problems in the program.

If the lesson is a program you created, revise it according to the errors discovered. If it is a commercial program, consider if it is still usable with your students. If you have designed your computer lesson on paper, students can try out the paper examples and practice items, to help you revise your program *before* you have it coded into the computer.

Summary

This chapter outlines the basic procedures for programming a concept learning lesson, where "programming" is the development of the computer lesson on paper without coding it into the computer via a programming language. For most concept learning lessons, a definition and best example provide the initial steps of instruction, followed by an easy-to-hard sequence of example presentation, followed by practice exercises that use the same easy-to-hard sequence. Practice feedback is styled to match the different kinds of answers that a student may give: right, wrong, and unanticipated. Lesson strategies used can be tutorials, games, simulations, or problem solving tools.

Screen displays are the final step to complete the lesson, since adequately prepared screen displays outline both the lesson content and sequence, and can be used by the programmer to construct the CAI lesson. As with any new instructional materials, the lesson should be evaluated by several learners before it is implemented in the classroom.

While the body of this chapter focuses on concept learning methods, these same methods are generally applicable for teaching other intellectual skills, such as rule using and problem solving. However, both rule using and problem solving have special instructional methods that should be used in CAI: special ways of stating the objective, presenting information and examples, and providing practice and feedback. These special methods are discussed in the next two chapters.

Chapter 5

Programming a CAI Lesson
for Rule Learning

Characteristics of Rules and Rule Learning

Overview

When we speak of rules, we mean more than regulations or laws that someone should follow. Rules are specific procedures or techniques that people use to solve problems. There are rules for dividing fractions, for changing a tire on a car, and for choosing a business suit. Some rules are a specific set of steps that we are to follow to solve a problem, such as rules for dividing fractions or changing a tire. Others are more like rules of thumb that are guidelines or principles for how we should operate. "Don't wear plaids with stripes" is a principle (rule) of dress, and "capitalize the first word of a sentence" is one of grammar. Like concepts, rules are intellectual skills that we commonly use at school, work, or at home.

Rules help us to solve problems by giving us specific directions on how to behave. Rules are like problem solving skills, in that they are used to solve problems. However, rules are different from problem solving in that they are specific methods that apply to specific problems. Problem solving methods are more complex skills that are used to solve broader and more complex problems. For example, there are grammar rules for writing a story, but writing a story is itself a more complex problem solving behavior than following rules. Problem solving skills require the learner to select and use rules in creative ways to solve problems.

Definition

Rules are specific procedures or techniques used to solve a class of problems. The problems usually have specific and identifiable solutions, and can be solved by correctly applying the rule to the problem. Rules may be *procedures or techniques* that have a series of sub-steps that must be accomplished in sequence to correctly apply the rule. They may also be single-statement *rules of thumb or principles* to guide one's behavior in solving a specific problem.

Rule Behaviors

A person has learned a rule when he or she can:

Demonstrate how to make withdrawals with a computer banking card.

Use commas correctly to separate independent and dependent clauses.

Apply Robert's Rules of Order to call on people at a meeting.

Utilize the principle of commutativity to exchange variables in an equation.

Convert Fahrenheit to Celsius temperatures using the formula $5F - 9C = 160$.

Learned Behaviors That Are Not Rules

Reciting or stating a rule (this is verbal information).

Identifying the type of rule that must be applied (this is concept learning).

Solving complex problems such as designing a science fair project (this is usually problem solving).

Solving problems in creative or original ways, such as inventing a musical theme or composing a poem.

Self-Check: Test Your Knowledge of Rules

1. Think of some examples of rules:

    Can you think of some that are part of your job?

    Can you think of some step-by-step rules that are procedures?

    Can you think of some rule of thumb principles?

2. Check to make sure that the examples are rules:

    Do users actually apply the rules, not just state them?

    Are they used to solve problems?

    Are they used on specific problems with a specific solution?

    Can the rule or method be stated?

3. Check your lesson objective and sub-objectives from your part 1 lesson map. Are you really teaching rules? If students simply repeat the description of a rule, you are teaching verbal information. If the rule cannot be stated or described, it may be because the method is too complex, which makes it a problem solving skill, not rule using. These outcomes are described in chapter 3 and 6.

Rule Learning

A person has learned a rule when he or she can apply it to solve a set of problems that vary in difficulty. Rule learning is not measured by a person's ability to describe or repeat the rule, although doing so may be a sub-skill that helps someone learn the rule. In some cases, a person learns a set of related rules all at once, such as learning a set of rules for punctuation. In this case, the learner must also learn how to *choose* the applicable rule for a problem from a set of rules, to identify cases where the specific rule applies. In these instances, the learner not only learns how to apply a specific rule, but when to apply it.

Lesson Components for Rule Learning

Overview

Most rule lessons should contain these lesson components:

the objective and purpose of the lesson

a description of the rule and/or its sub-steps

an example of its application

an explanation of how the rule is applied

examples of misapplications of the rule, and/or warnings of how the rule may be misapplied

(for sets of rules) instructions on how to choose the appropriate rule for a given problem

practice items where the student must use the rule to solve a problem

feedback that explains how a student missed a practice item, or why the answer was correct.

These lesson components assume that the student does not know anything about the rule. In these cases, students are given a lesson that teaches them all the lesson components, such as a deductive or inductive tutorial. Tutorial lesson strategies are explained in the next section of this chapter. If the student has already learned something about rules, a drill, simulation, or game may use some of the components listed above to refine the student's learning. These other strategies are also outlined in this chapter, in "CAI Lesson Strategies."

The lesson components will be sequenced differently in different rule lessons, depending upon the teaching strategy used. In some cases, you may present the rule to the student and follow it with examples (deductive tutorial). In other cases, you may present examples first and have the student infer the rule (inductive tutorial). If you have already taught the rule and examples in class, you may have the student just practice the application of the rule, which calls for practice and feedback strategies such as games or drills.

In the next section, we describe how to identify the important rule learning lesson components, and how to incorporate them in your lesson. First you will determine the components you need to give the student. Then you will select a strategy that delivers these components. We begin by looking at each of the lesson components for rule learning.

Rule Objectives

Why Do It: The Effectiveness of
CAI Lesson Objectives

Introducing the lesson content and goals is an important part of any CAI lesson. As learning research indicates, the introduction of the lesson can help students recall lesson-relevant prior knowledge and/or prepare for the new lesson.

One of the best ways to introduce the lesson is to explain the objective of the lesson. Students who know the objective of the lesson organize what they learn toward that objective. In addition, the objective can be followed by a short explanation of the purpose or function of learning the objective, if the purpose is not obvious to the student. Understanding the utility of the CAI lesson has demonstrably increased the motivation and learning of lesson content in students, especially for adult learners.

How to Do It: Presenting
Lesson Objectives

Informing the learner of the objective. The key to writing a successful lesson objective is to be as accurate as possible in the description of the objective. The objective should not be a statement of lesson content (e.g., "this lesson is about nouns"). Instead, the objective should describe what students will learn to do when they have learned the rule(s) that are the learning outcome of the lesson.

In this lesson you will learn to apply the Salami Principle of time management to organize a daily activity list.

After completing this lesson on temperature conversion, you will convert Fahrenheit temperatures to Celsius, and vice versa.

Informing the learner of rule sub-objectives. In addition to objectives, you can also include a statement of the sub-objectives of the rule learning objective, which are usually the sub-steps of the rule:

To apply the Salami Principle, you will learn to:

1. Identify a large scale task

2. Slice the task into "bites"

3. Estimate the time for a "bite"

4. Schedule each "bite."

The sub-objectives can be listed along with the major objective in the lesson introduction. Statements of sub-objectives are best used when there are a moderate number of them (five or fewer), and not a long list.

You Do It: Define Objectives
and Sub-objectives

1. Write down the major objective of your rule lesson, as you want the students to see it in your lesson:

_____

_____

_____

2. You can also include a statement or list of the sub-objectives of the lesson, which are the means to learn the major objective. These sub-objectives should reflect the sub-outcomes that you outlined for your lesson map in part 1 of this book:

_____

_____

_____

Self-Check on Objectives

Does your objective tell the learners that they will apply or use a principle or rule?

Does your objective state the context or subject in which the rule will be applied?

If you listed sub-objectives, are they skills and knowledge that must be learned in order to master the main objective?

Explaining the Purpose of the Lesson

Why Do It: Purpose Statements
as Motivators

When students know the value or function of what they are learning, it tends to increase their motivation to learn the lesson objectives. This motivational effect is particularly prevalent with students who are at or near the adult level.

How to Do It: Composing a
Statement of Purpose

If an explanation of the purpose or function of the lesson objective is used, it should be included beneath the statement of objectives and/or sub-objectives, although this explanation can go on a separate computer screen:

```
Once you have learned to use the
Salami Principle, you will be able
to effectively organize your daily
work schedule.
```

```
Learning to convert temps.
will help you master the
next lesson on laboratory
measurement.
```

You Do It: State the Lesson Purpose

Write in a short explanation of the purpose or function of the lesson, as students would see it on the computer screen:

Purpose/Function:

_____

_____

Self-Check on Lesson Purpose

Does your purpose statement appeal to learners' interests/motivation?

Does your message seem sincere and convincing, or does it seem as it you are trying to "sell" the lesson?

Presenting the Rule and Rule Sub-steps

*Why Do It: The Importance of
Presenting the Rule*

A concise and clear statement of the rule, coupled with an example of its application, is an excellent way to introduce the rule to the student. The statement of the rule explains how to use the rule, and the example clarifies how the rule is used. The student is thus given two complementary information sources for learning the rule, which increases the likelihood of rule understanding and retention.

If a lesson contains several related rules (such as rules for multiplication and division), consider presenting explanations of each rule together on the same screen, or at least immediately following one another. The presentation of related rules together allows the student to compare the common and distinguishing characteristics of each rule, which can clarify each individual rule and prevent confusions between rules. However, if the rules are presented together on the same screen, examples cannot usually fit in with them. If coordinate rules are presented separately, examples can be presented on the screen with each rule. Both simultaneous and successive methods may be effective, so choose the method that best fits the content of your lesson and makes sense.

How to Do It: Presenting the Rule and
Providing Learning Guidance

There are several ways in which the rule can be presented in the lesson. These are presented below.

Present the rule as a simple statement. This is best when the rule is relatively simple, and has no sub-steps:

```
All days of the week

and seasons of the year

are capitalized.
```

```
To store your computer lesson,

hit the "K" key and the "D"

key simultaneously.
```

Break the rule into sub-steps. Many rules are more complex than one-sentence statements. These rules require the student to perform several operations to apply the rule to solve a problem. In these cases, break the rule into sub-steps, and enumerate each one:

```
The Salami Principle involves the
following steps:

  1. Find a task that will take at least
  several hours of your time.

  2. Break the task up into several
  component tasks, each of which is
  no longer than an hour.

  3. Insert the component tasks into
  your daily schedule, wherever there
  is a gap at least 10% longer than the
  anticipated task time.
```

```
To convert Celsius to Fahrenheit (or vice
versa):

1. Remember the formula 5F - 9C = 160

2. Take the given temperature and multiply
   it times its factor in the formula

3. Solve the equation for the unknown,
   which is either F or C
```

You Do It: Create the Rule Presentation

For each rule objective and sub-objective, create a series of screens that describes the rule and how to use it. Where possible, have several rules presented together at once. If the rule has sub-steps, present each one in a clear and distinct manner:

Screen Sequence 1 (rule and rule sub-steps):

Self-Check on Rule Presentation

Is the rule stated in students' language?

Are sub-steps defined and clearly indicated?

Demonstrating the Rule

Why Do It: Demonstrations as Explanations

After the rule is presented, an example of its application should be presented along with the rule statement, or immediately following it. The example should show or explain how the rule is applied to solving the problem in question. When students see a demonstration of the rule, they remember the example and use it later as a guide when they apply the rule. Seeing an application also helps clarify any misunderstandings they may have about the verbal statement of the rule.

How to Do It: Selecting and Presenting Examples

There are several ways of presenting the application of the rule. These are presented below.

Select a best example. The "rule" for selecting an example is to start with a best example of the rule's application. A "best" example is one that is easy and familiar to the student; a prototypical example. As the lesson proceeds, more difficult examples can be given to the students or given as practice, but it is best to start with a simple, easy example.

Best example

```
When it is 5 Celsius outside, the
Fahrenheit equivalent is:

     5F - 9C = 160

     5F - 9(5) = 160

     5F - 45 = 160

     5F = 205

     F = 41
```

Show how rule steps are applied to the example. When an example application is presented, the steps or sub-steps of the rule can frequently be included next to the example, so that the student understands how the rule is applied. This is an effective technique to use, if the example and sub-steps fit on the same screen.

Example with sub-steps

```
        When it is 5 Celsius outside,
        the Fahrenheit equivalent is:

5F - 9C = 160        (write out the formula)

5F - 9(5) = 160      (plug in the given temp.)

5F - 45 = 160
                     (solve for the
5F = 205              unknown temp.)

F =  41
```

Use a sequence of screens for complex examples. Sometimes, the application of a rule results in a lengthy example, one that will not fit onto the computer screen. In such cases, consider a sequential demonstration of how each individual step is applied:

```
Breaking down a task into component tasks
(Step 2) can be done as follows:

TASK: Write up final report. (EST. TIME:
      5-6 Hours):

 Task 1 - Outline Content (1 hr.)

      2 - Write Introduction (1/2 hr.)

      3 - Compose Main Report (2 1/2 hr.)
            activities - 1 hr.
            problems - 1 hr.
            plans - 1/2 hr.

      4 - Write Up Summary (1 hr.)
```

This example of step 2 of the Salami Principle could be shown on one computer screen, with steps 1 and 3 on the preceding and succeeding screens.

Show another application of the rule. After a simple demonstration of the application of the rule, consider showing another application. This time, the example should be a little more complex or unfamiliar than the preceding one.

```
When the temperature is 10 Fahrenheit,
the Celsius equivalent would be:

    5F - 9C = 160

    5(10) - 9C = 160

    50 - 9C = 160

    -9C = 110

     C = -12.2
```

You Do It: Compose the Rule Presentation

For each of the rules in your lesson, write out an explanation of the rule's steps and/or sub-steps, and at least one example of its application. Try to keep the screen from becoming too wordy (see chapter 8). As we have just seen, there are several presentation options that you can choose and combine to teach each rule:

1. Present a simple statement of the rule.

2. Present the rule and sub-steps of the rule.

3. (For multiple rules) present the rules simultaneously.

4. Provide a simple example of the rule's application with/without sub-steps' application indicated.

5. Provide successively more complex examples.

6. (For lengthy rules) provide examples of the application of each rule sub-step.

Each rule lesson should contain some form of rule presentation with an example. The methods you choose should depend on the content of the lesson and the complexity of the rules.

Screen Sequence 1 (rule statement/steps):

Screen Sequence 2 (examples/explanations):

Self-Check on Demonstration

Is the demonstration example familiar to the student?

Have you clearly indicated how rule sub-steps are applied?

Providing Practice for the Learner

Why Do It: The Importance of Practice

Students best learn rules when they have the opportunity to practice the application of that skill. Consequently, rules are best learned when the student is provided with a certain amount and variety of practice problems. Through practice, students learn how to apply the rules and rule sub-steps to solve problems, and to affirm to themselves that they have learned to properly apply the rules. Thus, designing practice examples involves creating a sequence of exercises that guide the application of the rules to various examples, to the point where students can be sure they know how to easily use the rules to a varied set of problems.

To make rule learning practice especially effective, some careful thought should be given to the type and sequence of practice examples given. Research has shown that students who *practice* on a wide range of problems are better at *solving* a wide range of problems.

How to Do It: Designing Items to
Elicit Student Performance

Almost all rule using practice involves presenting a practice problem for the student that requires some application of the rule:

```
For the following project,
use the Salami Principle to
create a schedule of sub-tasks:

(project description)
```

```
When the temperature is 27
Fahrenheit, what is its
Celsius equivalent?

Type in the number of its
Celsius equivalent.
```

However, designing good rule practice involves more than simply writing down a problem. Creating CAI rule practice involves:

1. Deciding on the number and type of practice items.

2. Choosing an answer format, such as multiple-choice or short answer.

3. Choosing the various types of answers that will be accepted as correct.

4. Composing a practice frame that accommodates the CAI screen.

In the next several pages, we take each of these four steps in order, and explain how they should be used to design CAI practice. Then, you will design your own practice frames in the last section of this chapter.

Decide on the number and type of practice items. The first step is to decide how many practice exercises you want to include in your lesson. Since students should practice on a number of different problems, at least two problems should be included, and probably more than that.

The problems you design should vary in both subject matter and difficulty. In designing problems that vary in subject matter, it is best to start with content that is more familiar to the student, and move to the more unfamiliar. Then, too, the first problems should be the easiest, with more difficult problems following.

Finally, you may want to provide a few extra practice exercises for students who may have difficulty in correctly answering your exercises. The computer can "count" the number of times it takes a student to get the correct answer to a problem, and how many problems the student missed the first time. On the basis of the student's error record that is kept by the computer, the student can be given extra problems to work on, usually in an easy-to-hard sequence. This form of remedial instruction will be explained more in the next section, but you should decide now if you want to have such supplementary exercises.

Choose an answer format. After deciding on the type of problem exercises, you need to decide how you will ask the student to answer each exercise. There are two basic answer formats for CAI: (1) the student chooses the correct answer from the options you provide, (2) students compose their own open-ended answers.

<table>
<tr><td align="center">*Answer-option format*</td><td align="center">*Short-answer format*</td></tr>
<tr><td>

```
What is the Fahrenheit equivalent
of 12.2 Celsius?

   a) 10        b) 14

   c) 23        d) 8

Type in the LETTER of the correct
answer and press RETURN.
```

</td><td>

```
When the temperature is -12.2
Celsius, it is _____ degrees
Fahrenheit.




Type in the NUMBER of your answer
and press RETURN.
```

</td></tr>
</table>

When a student chooses from an answer option that you provide, it is a lot easier for the computer to judge whether an answer is correct or incorrect, and a lot easier for you to tell the computer what the correct and incorrect answers are, since the student must *choose* from preselected answers. However, some rule learning problems do not lend themselves to a multiple-choice format, such as our time management example, where the students must outline their own daily schedule of activities. In such cases, a short-answer format may be best.

If you choose an answer option format, be sure to include at least three "reasonable" options for the student to choose in addition to the correct answer. This will reduce the likelihood of students guessing the correct answer. Reasonable answer options are ones a guesser might choose as a correct answer. Other possible options are incorrect answers that result from a misapplication of the rule (getting 5F and 9C confused as 9F and 5C).

```
A 4-hour budget project should be divided
into at least ____ sub-projects.

a) 4          b) 8          c) 10

d) 9          e) 12         f) none of the above
```

If students are to be given a second chance at the problem if they get it wrong the first time, at least five or six options should be available in the exercise. Again, all incorrect answer options should be reasonable ones, ones that are not obviously incorrect.

If you choose a more open-ended answer format, one where the students will type in their own answers, try to make their responses as specific as possible, by asking for short responses:

```
When it is 55 Fahrenheit,
it is __C.
```

```
A 4-hour project can best be
broken down into at least ___
sub-projects.
```

If your problems require longer, more varied answers (such as our daily schedule answer for the time management problem), you should consider asking the student to compose his or her answer off screen, to be given to you for evaluation:

```
Using the task list just described,
complete a daily work schedule that
will allow you to complete all these
tasks that day.

Use a daily schedule log sheet in
the activities portfolio next to the
computer. When you complete the schedule,
submit it to your teacher.


   Press R to review task list . . .
   Press Return when schedule is turned
      in. . .
```

The problem answers can be shown to the teacher immediately after the problem is completed, or the student can complete all the problems on the computer and submit all the answers together. Note that the example allows for student review before answering.

Determine acceptable and unacceptable answers. The main point to this step is to decide what *versions* of a correct answer you will accept. If a student types in "1)" instead of "1" when choosing an answer option, is that acceptable? What if they type in "68 degrees" instead of "68" on a short-answer question? What if they answer "lincon" instead of "Lincoln?" Never underestimate the capability of students to respond in completely unanticipated ways, even when they know the right answer.

If you are using an answer-option format, the variety of correct answers is greatly reduced, but you should still prepare for students who will misinterpret instructions on how to answer.

The task of determining different versions of a correct answer is more complex when students creates their own answers to the problem, as opposed to choosing an option. As a general rule, the more words a student must enter for an answer, the tougher it is to anticipate all possible versions of a correct answer. Whenever possible, try to limit the student response to one or two words or numbers:

Possible Student Responses to a Question
That Has a Correct Answer of "23"

23
twenty-three
23 degrees
23 Fahrenheit degrees
23 Farenhiet degrees
twenny-three

When composing the problem exercises, you should invest some time in anticipating how students who know the correct answer may answer "incorrectly" and if these answers will be acceptable. These answers may include misspellings, lack of capitalization or punctuation, or even ballpark figures (e.g., 23 1/3 instead of 23 1/6).

Compose the practice frames. After you have determined the number and type of practice problems and the answer formats and correct answers, you are ready to compose the actual practice exercises for the computer. The two main concerns in writing the practice frames are: (1) writing clear directions to the student on how to answer the problem and (2) determining if the practice problem must be put on one or several computer screens.

In writing practice problem directions, be sure to include statements to the student that mention: (1) that this frame is a practice problem and (2) how he or she should answer the problem:

Problem directions

```
Now that you have seen how the Celsius-
Fahrenheit formula is applied, let's see
if you can use it to convert Celsius to
Fahrenheit, and vice versa:

When it is 16 Fahrenheit outside, it is
what temperature in Celsius?

    a) 22    b) -5    c) 14

    d) 0     e) 18

Type in the LETTER of your answer and
press RETURN.
```

In the preceding example, the statement at the top of the frame would explain that this is a problem exercise, and what the student is expected to do. The bottom statement provides instructions on how to answer the problem. More information on student directions will be provided in chapter 8.

Sometimes, the actual problem exercise will not fit onto one computer screen. In this case, you put sections of the problem on a series of computer screens, or make the exercise a paper-and-pencil project. If you put the problem on a series of screens, try to limit the problem to two to three screens, since students cannot see the problem all at one time. The second and third screen then have review functions that allow students to go back to the preceding problem screen. If possible, make each screen a problem *sub-set* of the problem as a whole, with its own question and answer segment for a sub-step of the overall rule.

Once all of your practice frames have been written, the next step is to plan the feedback that students will receive for their right and wrong answers to the exercises.

You Do It: Develop Practice Exercises

You will complete this activity after reading the next section of this chapter.

Providing Feedback to the Learner

*Why Do It: Feedback as a
Learning Experience*

"Feedback" is the knowledge of results that a student receives about practice performance. The computer "feeds back" a message to students about what they did and why it is right or wrong. Properly designed feedback messages allow students to correct any errors in their performance and affirm to themselves what they are doing right. Until students can know how they are wrong or that they are right, the learning they derive from practice is incomplete. Thus, the design of feedback can be just as important as the design of practice exercises.

Rule feedback is more than a simple message that tells students they answered the problem correctly or incorrectly. Good feedback tells students *how* they were wrong; how they misapplied the rule or the type of mistake they made. Feedback can also be provided for students who correctly answered the problem, to ensure that they fully understand the rule and its application. Feedback can also be provided for students who feel that they do not know enough to even try to answer the problem given them. This is a "help" type of feedback. In addition, feedback messages can vary with the number of tries the student has made on a problem; feedback for a student who has missed the third try at a rule problem is different from feedback he or she receives on the first miss at a problem.

The computer is a useful tool for rule feedback because it can send different feedback messages for different types of answers. Also, the computer can send students back to an exercise that they have missed, and count the number of times a student tries a particular exercise. It can even send a struggling student to a remedial or help module, to provide some additional instruction, and then send the student right back to the practice exercises. This ability to send students to previous exercises or new instructional sections is called the *branching* capability of the computer. It can be combined with feedback messages to produce a variety of computer responses to a student's practice performance.

How to Do It: Designing Feedback
for Rule Learning

To design proper feedback, you need to follow the steps below.

Decide how many times students will try to answer each practice exercise:

    i.   before you move them to another problem, or

    ii.   before you give them the answer, or

    iii.   before you give them help, or

    iv.   before you let them choose i-iii.
        (if you want to let them do that)

Compose individualize error messages, ones that explain the type of mistake the student made. Walk through each rule exercise and try to make the same mistakes your students would, misapplying the rule and rule sub-steps. Write an error message for each of the answers that would result from the mistake, explaining what the student did wrong. To handle completely unanticipated answers, include error messages such as "I don't understand your answer, read directions and try again."

Compose correct answer messages, ones that affirm and explain the application of the rule. The student who gets it right the second time can get a different message than one who gets it right the first time.

Decide where to branch (send) students if:

    i.   they are right on the first try

    ii.   they are right on the second/third try*

    iii.   they are wrong on the first try

    iv.   they are wrong on the second/third try*

    v.   they have no idea what they are doing*

    *these are optional tactics that you might or might not use in your lesson.

Do a dry run through the practice exercises to see if all the feedback messages and branches are in their proper places. Act like the student would, and try all combinations of right/wrong answers and number of tries that you anticipate in your program.

Feedback messages for different student responses

```
Very Good!

A 4-hour project can
be broken down into
at least 8 sub-parts.
Sub-projects should
be less than 1/2 hour.
```

(right first time)

```
No, not quite.

Remember that the
formula is:
5F - 9C = 160

Let's try again.
```

(wrong first time)

```
Not quite.

Let's review the
rule for scheduling,
and study an example
of how it's done.
```

(remedial frame for student wrong twice)

You Do It: Compose Practice and
Feedback Frames

Compose the practice and feedback frames for the CAI lesson, including any lesson "branches" on which a student will be sent. Write down each of your practice exercises on a sheet of paper, just as the student will see them on the computer screen. Use one page for each exercise. In composing your exercises, consider:

the proper amount and variety of practice problems, as well as an easy-to-hard sequence;

a multiple choice vs. open-ended response format;

clear explanations to the student about how to answer the problem; and

possible remedial instruction or practice frames for students who are having difficulty with the problems.

Take another sheet of paper for each problem exercise created, and draw a line to divide the paper in half.

A. On one side of the paper, list all versions of the correct answer that would be acceptable to you, including misspellings, lack of capitalization, etc. These versions would be the possible entries by the student into the computer. You may also want to list any "close but wrong" answers as well.

B. On the other side of the paper, list all the different feedback messages that you will use for the different types of answers that the student will give. This would include feedback for right and wrong answers, first and second tries, close but wrong answers, and even feedback for those who are totally lost.

C. If students are to be branched back or over to other parts of the lesson, depending on their answers, you should describe their destination. For example, if they are sent back to an earlier part of the lesson, you should write something like "if answer is wrong on second try, send back to start of lesson 1."

Screen Sequence 1 (practice frames):

Screen Sequence 2 (correct answer feedback frames):

Screen Sequence 3 (feedback for incorrect answer frames):

Self-Check on Practice and Feedback

Have you included a number and variety of practice problems for each rule and rule sub-step?

Have you included diagnostic error messages for incorrect answers?

Do you have feedback for unanticipated responses? For students who are totally lost?

Have you walked through the program several times to check the completeness of your branching routines and error messages?

Learning Strategies for Rule Learning

*Why Do It: Strategies Facilitate
Rule Learning*

Rule learning requires the learner to comprehend one or more propositions. Propositions state a relationship between two or more concepts. For example, "force equals mass times acceleration" states a fundamental proposition or rule in physics. This seemingly simple statement actually involves a couple of propositions. It involves the relationship of force to mass and acceleration. The relationship is "equals." This equation then involves propositions about force, mass, acceleration, and equality. Rules state relationships between concepts. Often, those relationships are based upon other concepts and relationships.

Learning strategies are activities that will help the learner understand the propositions that make up rules, not just the rule being taught, but skills that can be applied to all rule learning. Learning strategies, as we mentioned in the verbal information and concept chapters, help students learn how to learn. These strategies consist of generalizable learning skills that can be applied to all rules. They are different from the practice items and feedback describe in the previous sections. The practice items help learners to use the specific rule/principle being taught. Learning strategies, on the other hand, help learners to learn rules in general. Learning strategies that facilitate rule learning are those that help learners understand the relationships implied by the rule's propositions. Each of the learning strategies that we describe requires learners to access prior knowledge and relate it to the rules being learned. Therefore, they are said to be "generative," because they require learners to generate meaning for content by relating it to what they already know.

How to Do It: Embedding Rule
Learning Strategies in CAI

A variety of learning strategies can be used to help learners understand rules. The first is a simple verbal information strategy to help learners recall the steps of a complex rule. The next two help the learner understand the propositions implied by rules.

Use mnemonics to remember rule sub-steps. When you choose to enumerate the steps of a rule, you may want to compose a mnemonic (memory aid) that will help students remember the rule. You can also ask students to compose a mnemonic themselves:

| *Teacher-provided mnemonics* | *Student-generated mnemonics* |

```
Whenever you use the Salami Principle,
don't forget to use the FBI method:

1.Find a task that will take at least
several hours of your time.

2.Break the task up into several
component tasks, each of which is
no longer than an hour.

3.Insert the component tasks into your
daily schedule, wherever there is a gap
at least 10% longer than the anticipated
task time.
```

```
It is important that you remember the
formula 5F - 9C = 160. Try to think of
some jingle or mental picture that you
can attach to the formula, such as "the
5 Fords and 9 Chevys made  a 160 degree
turn. . .," and/or an image of these cars
turning. These are memory tricks that can
help you remember the formula.
```

Provide analogies or generate analogies. Analogies are hard on students. They force the learner to think. But that is exactly what we want them to do. Analogies require learners to explicitly relate new propositions to prior knowledge. An analogy consists of two propositions, each with two concepts. One of the propositions is incomplete.

Celsius is to *Fahrenheit*

as *Meter* is to _____

Propositions require that the learner determine the relationship between the two concepts in the complete proposition and to generalize that relationship to the other proposition. In the second, the learner must find the concept that completes the proposition with the one concept. The learner must decide what relationship Shakespeare has to the sonnet and what type of literature can be applied to e. e. cummings. It is important that learners can complete the second proposition; that is, that their prior knowledge contains the relationship. Otherwise, they will not be able to complete the analogy. After providing analogies for the learners, you may want them to generate their own. Give them the first proposition and let them generate their own related proposition from their own prior knowledge.

Salami Principle is to *a task*

as _____ is to _____

This sort of activity is even more generative. Learners need to figure out the relationship and draw specifically on their own prior knowledge to provide "gas is to car," "food is to body," and so on. The composer can evaluate responses and provide feedback.

Networking strategy. A person's memory comprises a giant network of related ideas. The connections or links between ideas form propositions. The purpose of a networking strategy is to identify the important ideas in a content area and to have the learner classify the nature of the relationships implied by the links between the important concepts. The designer identifies the important concepts in a content area, then presents those to the learner in pairs. The learner is required to classify the relationship between the two. Understanding the relationship between concepts helps the learner to understand the propositions which comprise the rules. For example, it is important to understand the relations between steps/problems of a rule. In addition to classifying relationships, you may also want the learners to identify the relationship of sub-steps and concepts in a rule lesson.

```
                    How are these related?

        A prioritize tasks      B subdivide tasks
        *********************************************
            1   A is the same as (equal to) B.
            2   A is similar to or like B.
            3   A is the opposite of B.
            4   A describes or identifies B.
            5   A is an example of B.
            6   A is a part of B.
            7   A and B are examples of the same thing.
            8   A precedes B in a sequence or process.
            9   A follows B in a sequence or process.
           10   A causes B to happen.
           11   A results from or happens because of B.
           12   A supports or documents B.

    Which number best describes the relationship between A and B?__
```

They might do this as they read through the material. Identify one function key or provide a response option for recording concepts as learners proceed through the lesson. The program will then take those concepts and present them to learners in a paired fashion to classify, as illustrated in the screen. This networking strategy has been shown to be an effective learning strategy. It motivates students to think about the rules they learn.

You Do It: Select a Lesson Strategy

Review the preceding lesson strategies and select one or more that you can embody into your rule lesson program. Put these strategies into your lesson by rewriting some of the lesson frames you have already completed, or by adding frames to your rule presentation.

Screen Sequence 1 (learning strategies frames for rule and rule sub-steps):

Self-Check on Learning Strategies

Can your strategy be used easily by students? Is it easy for them to understand?

Do you have a strategy to make rule sub-steps more memorable and understandable?

Selecting a Lesson Strategy

Why Do It: Lesson Strategies for Different Instructional Purposes

As indicated at the outset of the last section, certain instructional components, such as rule statements, examples, and demonstrations, are necessary to learn rules. These all help a student learn a rule and apply it. However, these lesson components can be embodied in different types of computer teaching strategies. Also, in cases where the student has already learned the rule, certain strategies may omit some lesson components.

The tutorial teaching strategy is an extremely popular method, one that includes all of the lesson components of the previous section. However, there are other computer strategies that can be used, such as simulations, games, drill and practice, or problem solving tools. Simulations, games, and drill and practice require that learners apply the rules they have learned to a number and variety of problems. Problem solving tools are helping strategies that can be used to remediate and enhance a student's rule learning.

Inductive and deductive tutorials presuppose that the learner has little or no knowledge about the rules to be learned. Drills, games, and simulations presuppose that students have to some degree already learned the rule(s), or are presently learning it from some other source (a tutorial, a teacher, etc.). Thus, a rule game can be used after a student has learned a rule in a class, lecture or through a deductive tutorial. All of these strategies can be used by themselves, or in conjunction with each other. For example, a deductive tutorial can be followed by a simulation or game, for enhanced rule practice.

In this section, you will use a short, step-by-step guide to select the type of lesson strategy that you feel best suits your instructional needs. There are a variety of computer teaching strategies, and they have been designed to serve different instructional purposes. Therefore, it is important that you know your general lesson purposes before using the guide.

You Do It: Select a Lesson Strategy

Using the guide below, answer each question and move to the step indicated by your answer:

Step 1.   Does the lesson objective require learning to apply a rule?

If yes, go to step 3

If no, go to step 2

Step 2. Does one of the lesson sub-objectives require rule learning?

If it requires rule learning, go to step 3

If it does anot require rule learning, go to another chapter. You do not need a rule lesson. You may need a lesson on concepts or verbal information. Review the learning outcomes section in part 1.

Step 3. Have students already learned the rules of your lesson? Are they ready to try applying them to problems?

If they are ready to apply the rule, go to step 4

If they should learn the rules, go to step 6

Step 4. Do you want to first provide a review or practice of the rules, or do you want the learners to immediately try out the rules on new situations?

For review/practice, go to step 5

For transfer to new situations, go to step 9

Step 5. You need to develop a drill and practice lesson or a rule game. Go to the drill and practice and game sections of this chapter. Also, see step 10.

Step 6. Will the student need to apply the rule(s) to a wide variety of settings (school, home, work, etc.)?

For wide and varied applications training, go to step 7

For more specific situation training, go to step 8

Step 7. You need to construct a tutorial. An inductive tutorial may be best. Go to the tutorial section of this chapter. Also, see step 10.

Step 8. You need to construct a tutorial lesson, probably a deductive one. Go to the tutorial section of this chapter. Also, see step 10.

Step 9. You need to develop a rule simulation. Go to the simulations section of this chapter. Also, see step 10.

Step 10. Will you need to construct on-screen problem solving aids for students? These are aids to help students remember rules and how to apply them.

If you need such aids in your lesson, see the problem solving tools section after you have reviewed the strategy section you selected.

If you do not think you need these aids, go to the section you just selected.

This step-by-step guide is intended to help you select a teaching method for your computer lesson, and should not be regarded as law. Once you have previewed a strategy recommended by the guide, you may want to review other strategies as well, to compare them to your chosen strategy. For example, after reviewing the section on inductive tutorials, you may also want to review the deductive tutorials section, and utilize that strategy instead. In particular, do not forget that some of these strategies can be used together, such as a tutorial followed by a simulation or game. Almost any tutorial can have one of the other strategies piggybacked onto it, to enhance learning and application of the rule.

CAI Lesson Strategies

Tutorials

*Why Do It: Tutorials as Primary
Teaching Strategies*

Tutorials follow the teaching strategy that a tutor might use to teach rules. Tutorials are especially valuable when students have to learn the steps and application of new rules/principles before solving problems with them. Acting as a tutor, the computer has the student learn rules and their applications, and practice the rules.

Tutorials can be inductive or deductive. A deductive tutorial uses the computer to *present* rules and demonstrate their application. An inductive tutorial uses the computer to help the student *derive* (induce) the rules or principles of the lesson. The deductive method is easier to design, and more likely to produce rule learning in a shorter time. An inductive lesson may be remembered better, and the rules better transferred to new situations the learner encounters.

For certain rules, an inductive sequence may not be a good choice. This is because certain rules are too complex to be easily induced by the student. For example, a rule or principle that has over three sub-steps might be difficult for a student to induce, and it might be difficult for a teacher to design an inductive lesson for it. Many mathematical or geometric principles may be too difficult for the student to induce, and as such it may be better to show a student the principle via a deductive tutorial. Inductive tutorials may best suit simple rules that involve only one or two steps. Also, simpler principles such as "hot air rises" may be easy to induce. The best rule of thumb for the design of inductive tutorials may be to try to do it, but be prepared to "go deductive."

How to Do It: Constructing a Deductive Tutorial

Deductive tutorials can be constructed by following all of the lesson components and procedures outlined in the lesson components section. The tutorial should involve:

1. Presenting the rule objective/sub-objectives.

2. Presenting the rule and its sub-steps (if applicable).

3. Demonstrating an application of the rule, with explanations.

4. Presenting rule practice in an easy-to-hard sequence, with branching.

5. Presenting feedback for correct and incorrect answers.

The practice and feedback sections can also incorporate elements of games or simulations (see following sections of this chapter). That is, the practice can be done as a game or simulation, or a game/simulation can be added onto the lesson to enhance the initial lesson practice.

You Do It: Construct a Deductive Tutorial

Go back to the lesson components section of this chapter, and follow each of the steps outlined to construct lesson components for rule learning. Make sure that all of these are in a presentational mode: that they are being shown to the student. For each one of the activity portions of this section, construct a series of computer screens on paper that convey that lesson component. The completed lesson should have the following components:

rule objective(s)

statements and descriptions of rule and its steps

applications with explanations

sequenced practice

feedback for the type of wrong and right answer given

By following the *You Do It* activities in the lesson components section, you should have a rough draft of a deductive tutorial.

How to Do It: Constructing an Inductive Tutorial

To construct an inductive rule tutorial, present the rule applications at the beginning of the lesson, and have students generate the rule from the applications given. This is done by questioning the student about the application. The lesson will pose questions to students about each example they see, using a series of questions to help students induce the rule or principle. Most inductive sequences follow the strategy presented below.

Describe the purpose and method of the inductive lesson. Tell students how to answer the questions or problems you have given to them. You can include an explanation of why you want them to induce the rule:

```
In this lesson you will be given
some examples of problems and their
solutions. You will have to figure
out the rule used to solve the problem.
By figuring out the rule yourself, you
will understand it better.
```

Present a simple example of the application of the rule, and ask students how it is solved. As an alternative, you can give students a general description of the rule, and cue them to determine its characteristics or steps:

```
John has a two-hour reporting task.
He has organized it as follows:

1. Write report draft (1-2:30)
2. Edit draft (4-4:30)

John has used the "Salami Principle"
to organize his time. What do you think
this principle does to a task?
```

```
The first principle of time
management is the Salami
Principle.

     (Salami Graphic)

What do you do with a big
salami you can't eat all
at once (hint: use a knife)?
```

Provide immediate feedback to the learners on their answers. For wrong answers, make your feedback as supportive as possible, and try to give students a second chance (with hints) before telling them the rule. For right answers, you can follow up the feedback with another question, one that requires them to induce more information about the rule:

```
Righto! John has divided up the task
into smaller bites or sub-tasks. It's
like slicing up a big salami into smaller
bites.

Next question: why do you slice up a
salami into smaller bites?
```

```
No, not quite. Think of it
this way.

        (GRAPHIC)


What would you do with the
knife to make a sandwich?
```

For some examples/questions, student replies may be quite varied, so that it is difficult for the computer to judge them. In these cases, design the lesson so that the students' answers are not judged by the computer. Instead, provide them with feedback on what their answer should resemble. If the student is doing the lesson with other students or a teacher, you can have them evaluate the answer off-screen:

```
Your answer should be that
John is dividing up the big
task into smaller tasks.

It's like dividing up a
big Salami.

Next question: why do you
cut up a big salami?
```

```
Your answer:
"slice up the salami"

Leave your answer on the
screen and go get the teacher
to look at it.  If you can't
get the teacher, write your
answer down and go on.
```

In cases where there are several sub-steps to the rule, you can have the student induce one of the steps in the rule, and then another sub-step as a separate problem:

```
After you have divided the task
up into smaller bites, what do
you think you do next?  Hint: on
a real salami you would estimate
how thick each slice is.
```

After the student has induced a rule, provide practice and feedback problems in the manner described in the lesson components section. For rules with several sub-steps, you can provide a short practice problem after each sub-step:

```
As you may have determined, the
the next step is to estimate the
amount of time for each sub-task.

Suppose you had to write a 500-
word paper? How many minutes
would the sub-task "review a
draft" take??
```

After the rule is induced, provide the student with practice and feedback, as described in the lesson components section in this chapter.

In some cases, both inductive and deductive methods can be used in the same tutorial. For example, you can have the student induce the general or basic rule and receive further explanation of the rule in the lesson. For lengthy or complex rules, this tactic is often necessary.

You Do It: Compose an Inductive Tutorial

Beginning with a screen that describes the lesson purposes, construct a draft of an inductive rule lesson. Take each rule or principle of the lesson, construct a simple application of the rule, and develop a series of screens that question the student about the rule or principle. Be sure to include feedback frames for wrong answers to the questions. Finally, include practice and feedback problems.

Screen Sequence 1 (purpose and directions):

Screen Sequence 2 (problems/examples of rules with inductive questions):

Screen Sequence 3 (feedback to students on their inductions):

Screen Sequence 4 (practice and feedback frames):

Games

Why Do It: Games as Motivating Practice

Many students' first and most pleasant experiences with a computer have been with computer games. Computer games are an established part of younger students' recreations and diversions. They have two instructional strengths for rule learning. First, they can be motivating and captivating to a student, regardless of age, because they embody elements of competition and challenge. Second, the game format suits different types of problem solving activities, since the solution of a problem or problems is often the basis for doing well in a game. For instruction, computer games can challenge students to use rules and principles to solve problems in a competitive environment. As a caution, teachers should be careful to make sure that a computer game does require application of rules or principles, and is not just an entertainment device. Also, games should not be a debilitating experience for slower learners or ones with a low self-concept; there should be some provision for all learners to "make some points" or play at their own level.

For rule learning, games should have students apply the rules they have learned to a number and variety of problems. Like drill and practice, games are best used to enhance rules students have already learned through computer tutorials or classroom instruction. Games can be used as a substitute for standard drill and practice routines. They can be incorporated as part of a tutorial lesson, or they can be used as a separate practice module. However, unless the game provides extensive instructive feedback on student answers, it cannot replace the practice and feedback elements of a good deductive or inductive tutorial.

All rule games should require a variety of rule application exercises. The variety of exercises can help students apply rules to problems with varying degrees of difficulty. To maintain the spirit of gamesmanship, the lesson should include scorekeeping, levels of difficulty, and achievement levels/awards.

How to Do It: Constructing
a Rule Game

At the outset, tell the student the purposes and rules of the game. Students can be told the objectives of the game, and its relation to previous rule lessons/instructions:

```
Conversion Challenges

In this lesson you will practice
converting temperature from
Fahrenheit to Celsius.

You will use the conversion rules
you learned in Science Module #4
```

```
The object of this game is to
get 100 pts. as quickly as you
can, with the least number
of tries.

3-5     tries = Genius
6-9     tries = Wizard
10-12   tries = Novice
```

If possible, give the students a choice of topics and/or competitive levels from which they can select:

```
What conversions would you like to
start with?

a. F to C?
b. C to F?
```

```
What degree of difficulty?

1. Easy   (10 pts. each answer)
2. Hard   (20 pts.)
3. Killer (35 pts.)
```

You can also allow the student to switch difficulty levels within the game.

Present a problem that requires application of the rule. Generally, it is a good idea to start with an easier problem (even if the student chooses a high level of difficulty), to get the student accustomed to the game. Make sure that you have a large pool of practice items. Some games have more than 100 exercises.

```
            Here's your first problem!
                 When it is 65 F,
  (GRAPHIC)      What is the C temp.?


                 # of tries = 0
                 score = 0
```

You can also keep the students updated on their progress, by recording and showing their scores.

Design feedback messages for student answers. This can be a simple right or wrong message followed by their score. However, this feedback is not as instructive or corrective as other types of diagnostic feedback. It is used when students should have already mastered the lesson. As an alternative, you can provide help frames with simple feedback for students:

```
        Sorry!


     65 F = 16 C

      # of tries = 1
         score = 0
```

```
  Sorry! Your answer was
  too high!!

  Would you like to try the
  problem again?

       RETURN to try again
       SPACE BAR for answer & new
       HELP to review formula
       Q to quit the game
```

For rule applications, it often helps to give students a second chance at applying the rule to a problem they missed.

Design an end point to the game. This can be when all problems have been tried, when the student has attained a certain score or number of attempts, or when the student chooses to quit the game. At any rate, the game should close with some summary of the student's performance. This can be a comparison to other students' performance, or scores, or some level of achievement:

```
Very GOOD! (GRAPHIC)

You scored 100 pts. on only 6
tries!!

This makes you a WIZARD.

You were only three tries off
the all-time record!
```

When constructing the game, there are some other strategies that you can build into the game, depending on the nature of the lesson content:

For complex rules, have students try rule sub-steps as the first part of the game. Later, move on to using all the sub-steps together.

"Jazz up" the game with graphics. Have the students solve problems with pictures in them, and have results graphically displayed.

Have the computer randomize the game problems that are given to the students, so no student gets the same order of problems. If there are levels of problem difficulty, the problems can be randomized within the levels without mixing them up across levels.

Have the computer record the scores and number of tries for each student, so you have a record of their achievement.

Have students do the rule games in small groups, and later do the game by themselves.

Allow students some way to leave the game at any point.

You Do It: Construct a Rule Game

Using the steps outlined above, construct the screens for your rule game, starting with the objectives and purpose of the lesson. Be sure to include an ample number of rule problems.

Screen Sequence 1 (objectives, purpose, directions, student choices):

Screen Sequence 2 (rule problems for each level of difficulty in program):

Screen Sequence 3 (feedback and remedial frames for all rule problems):

Screen Sequence 4 (summary/closing frames):

Simulations

Why Do It: Simulations for Rule Transfer

A simulation simulates a scenario or situation that the learner would encounter in real life. Rule simulations require the learner to apply rules or principles to a simulated problem. As such, simulations can promote the transfer of rules to real life situations. As an example, a time management simulation might recreate an office environment on the computer, in which students must decide how to schedule their office duties.

Simulations are used to enhance student rule learning. The student must already have learned the applicable rules or principles before beginning the simulation. Simulations can be an excellent supplement to a tutorial, because they may provide more extensive and complex rule practice than a tutorial practice and feedback segment. Because they require numerous decisions by the student, simulations maintain a high level of student interaction and interest.

The key feature of rule simulation instruction is that a problem scenario is provided which the student must act upon, and which changes with the decisions the student makes. Games and drills provide a number of separate rule problems for the student. Rule simulations create one problem scenario that changes through the course of the lesson. Often the changing real life scenario motivates the student to solve problems, and the reality of the scenario makes students feel that they are learning useful skills.

Simulations can be extremely complex to design and program, particularly where a student choice may simultaneously change a number of factors. Consequently, "How to Do It" in this section demonstrates how to construct a basic simulation, one that uses simplified real life scenarios.

How to Do It: Constructing a Rule Simulation

First, describe the objective and purpose of the situation. Indicate that the student will be making decisions in the lesson:

```
The Metric Homemaker

Trying to Survive in the
Metric Age.

(GRAPHIC)

In this lesson you will
use metric measurements
to maintain your home.
```

Wherever possible, permit students to choose their own starting point in the simulation:

```
What measurement unit
would you like to use
first?

    a. weight
    b. length
    c. temperature
```

```
Where would you like to
start?

    a. bedroom
    b. kitchen
    c. livingroom
```

Begin the simulation by presenting a problem scenario of which the student becomes a part. The student must choose some course of action. The scenario can be a trip, a job, a task, anything that will allow students to apply the rules/principles they learned:

```
O.K. You're in the kitchen.
What item would you like
to prepare?

a. ham      b. eggs
c. coffee   d. broccoli
```

```
You've got two eggs in the
pot.  What temperature do
you want to cook eggs?


(GRAPHIC)  Type in Celsius
           temp.
```

Have the scenario change to conform to the student's decision. The change should be based on the student's answer in such a way that the answer has *caused* the alteration. The new scenario should require further input from the student. The scenarios will change with individual student answers, but they must all present a problem that requires application of the rules/principles learned:

```
Oh! Oh! You set the eggs
at 0 C, which is freezing!

     (GRAPHIC)

Looks like your eggs are
in the freezer!

Choose a new C temp.
```

```
Now you've got the eggs
at 200 C.

     (GRAPHIC)

The pan is starting to
melt! Adjust the
temperature fast!!
```

Note that in many cases, the feedback for a choice is built into the scenario itself. That is, the way the scenario changes will inform students about the correctness of their choice.

The simulation should continue until some logical ending point is reached, one that conforms to the real life decisions the student makes. At that time, a summary judgment about student performance can be made:

```
You have now maintained every
room in the house.

     (GRAPHIC)

You started 1 fire and broke 2
pieces of furniture, but you're
still in one piece.
```

After a student completes a simulation, hold a "debriefing" session, where the student discusses the simulation with the teacher and/or classmates. You should ask questions like:

What was the toughest problem in the simulation?

How could you use these rules in real life?

You can also give written assignments as a debriefing.

There are a number of other features that you can build into simulations to make them more effective and interesting. A few are outlined below:

For more complex rules, the simulation can require the application of sub-steps of the rule as part of the early stages of the simulation, instead of the whole rule at once.

For many simulations, a light touch is preferable. Try to keep the simulation humorous, while maintaining a sense of reality.

Design the simulation so that students can exit the program if they wish, or start over again.

HELP frames can be designed so that students can preview the rules used in the simulation while they are doing it.

Design your simulation for group participation. For tougher rule problems, a group of two to four students can work on the problem together. Students find group simulations to be both effective and enjoyable.

You Do It: Design a Rule Simulation

Using each of the steps below, design a basic rule simulation. Before beginning, decide on the scenario, and the decision possibilities that students can make. If it seems too complex to design, look for a simpler scenario, or choose another strategy such as a game or drill.

Screen Sequence 1 (explanation of objectives, purpose, and scenario):

Screen Sequence 2 (student choice to enter scenario at a certain point):

Screen Sequence 3 (first scenario, possible second scenarios, and feedback based on choices made in first scenario, third scenario choices, etc.):

Screen Sequence 4 (end of simulation, summary comments):

Drill and Practice Routines

Why Do It: Drill and Practice
to Enhance Learning

Drill and practice routines are frequently used to enhance rule learning. Drills require extensive practice of previously learned rules, since they require the student to apply the rule to a number of problems. As such, they are effective complements to computer tutorials or classroom instruction.

A drill and practice strategy will administer a problem to a student, accept and evaluate the answer to the problem, judge it as correct or incorrect, provide feedback, and administer a new problem or repeat the old one. In many cases, the strategy also records the number of times a student missed a particular question and the total number of correct and incorrect answers, which a teacher can use to evaluate student progress.

Drill and practice routines are particularly suitable for problems that have specific answers, since it is easier to design problems, judge answers, and provide feedback for them. Addition, division, spelling, and grammar rules have all been used effectively in drill and practice routines. Similarly, principles such as physics laws may fit well into a drill. Rules that have require lengthy or complex problems, or vague problems, may be difficult to drill. While drills appear simple to construct, good routines can use a number of subtle techniques. A good rule drill should employ most or all of the following features:

A description of the purpose, objectives, and directions of the drill.

A practice sequence that requires problem solution through application of the rule, or its sub-steps.

Problems that vary in content and difficulty. The problems can increase in difficulty, or students can choose a difficulty level.

Feedback to students about the answers they missed, particularly feedback about how they misapplied the rule to the problem.

Review of practice items, where a missed problem is repeated immediately or later on in the drill.

Student recordkeeping, where the computer records and reports student performance to the teacher and/or student.

The essential purpose of the drill is to furnish the student with informed practice of rules learned. Drills are similar to the basic practice and feedback routines of tutorials, but are usually more extensive.

How to Do It: Constructing a Rule Drill

Begin the drill by giving the student an overview of the upcoming lesson, including the lesson objective/purpose, and directions on how to use the computer drill:

```
Drill 1: Temperature Conversion


This drill will help you learn
to convert Fahrenheit tempera-
tures to Celsius, and vice
versa.

To do this you will apply the
temperature conversion rules
you learned in the last lesson.
```

```
Directions


You will be given a
temperature in one
system, and will convert
it to another.

Some of these problems
will be tougher than
others.
```

If the rule practice can have a wide range of difficulty, you can have the students select a difficulty level. If the rules have a number of sub-steps, students can elect to start on sub-step practice:

```
Choose one of the
practice levels
to start:

1. easy
2. more difficult
3. difficult

You can switch levels
during the drill.
```

```
Where would you like to
start this drill?


1. writing the formula
2. converting to an unknown
3. solving conversions

Parts 1. and 2. are sub-steps
of the overall formula.
```

If you intend to compare students' drill performances you will want them all to start at the same level and problem. If not, they can choose levels and switch levels in the program by using a key like the ESCAPE key to return to the menu.

Present a drill problem to the student. You can have the students begin by solving problems that only require using a sub-step of the rule, or have them start using the rule as a whole:

```
Sub-step 1: Problem 1

Enter the formula to
solve for C when the
temperature is
      5 F?

Formula_____
```

```
Level 1: Problem 1

What is the Celsius
equivalent of
      8 F?

Enter number to one decimal.
```

In some cases, all students can begin with sub-step practice, while in others they can choose from a menu (see second step). If students have not been exposed to rule instruction for some time, the sub-step practice can be a useful refresher practice.

Present a series of rule problems to the student. Problems should vary in difficulty (even within difficulty levels), and should range across all contexts where the rule would be applied. Generally, you should use an easy-to-hard sequence of problems. As indicated in the third step example, all problems should be numbered so the students can track the number of problems they have done.

Present feedback messages for each drill problem. Some drills inform students that they were right or wrong, without any explanation. This is more suitable when you want to test students' rule learning in the drill. However, it is a good idea to explain how students misapplied the rule, or clue them about the nature of the correct answer:

```
Your answer: 60 F

Not quite. You may have
reversed the F and C conversion
numbers in the formula.

Press R to review formula.
```

```
Your answer: 80 C

Incorrect. Your answer
is too high, but you're
getting "warm"!!
```

Note that help can be provided for students who have missed the problem. This help can be statements of the rule and/or examples of its application.

Branch the students to the same or different problems after feedback. You should use several branching strategies depending upon students' answers and their number of tries. When students miss an item, either (a) give them the answer and give them a new problem, (b) tell them that or how they were incorrect and let them try it again, or (c) tell them that or how they were incorrect and have them try it again later, after three to six other drill items:

```
Your answer was 60 F

Not quite. You may have
reversed the conversion
numbers for the F and C
factors in the formula.

    Press R to review rule.
    RETURN to do problem again.
```

```
Your answer: 80 C

Incorrect. Your answer is
too high, but you're getting
"warm"!!!

Later, we'll try this problem
again.

RETURN for next problem.
```

As a rule, you should have students try the problem again, before telling them the answer. You can also arrange special branches for students who are doing well in the program. If they have solved a number of problems on the first try (particularly if they are difficult ones) the computer can "count" these answers/tries and send the student out of the program or into more difficult problems.

As a close to the drill, give students feedback about their overall performance. This can include number or percentage of problems correct, and the number of tries:

```
              Final Score:

    You solved 60% of easy probs.
    on the first try, 30% on second.

    You solved 40% of the difficult
    on the first try, 20% on second.

    Would you like to try again?
```

Where students have not completed most of the problems, have them try the drill again. As indicated, the computer can store students' performance record for you to look at later.

There are several other features that you can build into the drill to enhance its learning effectiveness:

The computer can randomize the presentation of problems, so that no student gets the same sequence. This can even be done within difficulty levels.

Vary the contexts of rule application in the problems. Can the rule be applied to work, school, home problems? If so, you may want to include problems from all of these contexts.

You Do It: Construct a Rule Drill

Beginning with the introductory drill screens, outline a drill and practice routine on paper. Begin with the introductory frames and move to the practice and feedback frames. Remember that drills require a large number of varied rule applications problems, and a variety of branches and feedback messages. The same screen can contain feedback and information about where the student will be branched.

Screen Sequence 1 (objectives, purpose, menu of choices):

Screen Sequence 2 (rule sub-step problems or rule problems, in an easy-to-hard sequence. Difficulty levels may be included):

Screen Sequence 3 (feedback and branching messages to student, with feedback designed to type of error in the solution or type of misapplication of the rule):

Screen Sequence 4 (remedial or help frames for errors):

Screen Sequence 5 (scores and summary feedback):

Problem Solving Tools for Rule Learning

Why Do It: Problem Solving Tools Aid
Acquisition and Application

Problem solving tools should not be confused with problem solving outcomes. Problem solving outcomes are specific types of learning outcomes that are different from concepts and rules. Problem solving tools are instructional aids that are used for all types of learning outcomes: rules, concepts, problem solving, even verbal information outcomes. These tools are instructional adjuncts to tutorials, games, simulations, and drills. They help students learn and practice a given learning outcome. For rules/principles, students use a problem solving tool to acquire the rule and apply it to problems.

Problem solving tools are embedded into the computer program itself. They help the student solve the "problem" of mastering the learning outcome. For rule learning, a tool for learning the rules of time management can be a checklist of guidelines for using the rules of time management. A similar checklist can be constructed to use metric conversion rules to solve conversion problems. In either case, the tools can be called onto the screen when students are trying to apply the rules to solve a problem. Similarly, a computer database can be a problem solving tool that stores and organizes the information that students need to apply rules to solve a problem.

Problem solving tools are useful aids. They provide the kind of on-screen help that a teacher might give to a student who was "stuck" on a problem. However, with a problem solving tool the student can get help anytime without leaving the computer program. As with many on-screen aids, the tool can model the way an expert would solve the problem, or the information an expert would use.

There are a wide variety of simple and sophisticated problem solving tools for computer lessons. For our purposes, we review one of the most basic and important tools for rule learning, the use of an on-screen aid.

How to Do It: Constructing a
Rule Learning Tool

A rule learning tool should help the student apply the rule. To do this, the aid can focus on reviewing the characteristics of a good solution. This can help students judge if they have applied the rule correctly, without telling them the answer:

```
        Time Management Checklist

        Does your solution have:

        o list of sub-tasks?
        o breaks between them?
        o all less than 1 hour?
```

Checklists are popular forms of on-screen aids. With a checklist, students are asked about their solutions, encouraging them to question themselves.

As an alternative to reviewing the solution characteristics, you can use an example of the application of the rule, similar to one shown in the lesson components section of this chapter:

```
        Application Example

        Task: review purchasing list
        Deadline: 3 days

        1. Estimate task time: 2 1/2 hrs
        2. Estimate available time: 6 hrs
        3. Sub-tasks
                Vendor check (45 min.)
                Price check (1 hour)
                Quantity check (45 min.)
```

Another alternative is to make an aid available that reviews the rule and its sub-steps. This would be similar to the rule presentation strategies outlined in the first part of the lesson components section.

Make the aid available to the student, to be called up during any rule applications practice. As an alternative, make the aid available only for initial applications of the rule, during the first two or three rule problems in a drill, tutorial, simulation, or game:

```
┌──────────────────────────────────────────┐
│                                          │
│                                          │
│     Problem # 2                          │
│                                          │
│     What is the Fahrenheit               │
│     equivalent of 0 Celsius?             │
│                                          │
│     Type in the number only_____         │
│                                          │
│     Press H to review                    │
│      before answering.                   │
│                                          │
│                                          │
└──────────────────────────────────────────┘
```

Students can review the aid before they try to solve the problem, and then come back to the same problem and apply the rule. If you have several aids designed for students (example review, sub-step review), have different keystroke choices for each one. For example, "Press H to review rule," "Press E to see an example," etc.

You Do It: Construct a Rule
Problem Solving Tool

Review the lesson's rules, sub-steps, and examples. Decide on an aid or aids that will help students when they are applying the rule to problems. If possible, organize the aid into an on-screen tool that will be part of the computer lessons. If it will not fit into the computer, make it available as a print accompaniment to the lesson.

Screen Sequence 1 (rule learning aid):

Screen Sequence 2 (other aids):

Using Database Management Tools to Aid Rule Learning

How to Do It: Using Databases to
Clarify Rule Applications

In the last section we reviewed several types of problem solving aids to facilitate rule learning. One particularly useful aid is a database system, used to store information about rules/principles. Database systems are useful when students must learn a number of related rules all at once, such as rules for addition, multiplication, and subtraction. The database can be used to store relevant information about the rule, such as the rule name, sub-steps, and applications.

A database is like an electronic filing cabinet. It stores collections of related information in a file called a record. Each type of information in the file is a separate field.

Two Records of a Database on Punctuation Rules

(Field 1)	Name: Period	Name: Comma
(Field 2)	Used to: end a sentence abbreviate	Used to: separate dependent and independent clauses.
(Field 3)	Example: John went home. Ms. Jones is here.	Example: She came and saw, but she did not conquer.
(Field 4)	Confused with: N/A	Confused with: semicolon

The structure of a database allows a student to search it quickly for all types of relevant information.

In rule learning, databases can be used to store a large body of rule information in one place, which the student can access all at once. This information can include "nice to know but not necessary" information about the rule, such as the origin of the rule, or exceptions/modifications to its application in special cases. In these cases, the database can store information that would not be given in the lesson itself, since that information might detract from the essential learning task.

A rule learning database can also involve the use of learning strategies by students to clarify rule steps and applications. This happens when the lesson requires the student to create a database about rules. Constructing a database encourages the student to organize and compare information about related rules or principles, thus clarifying their relationships to one another.

How to Do It: Creating a Database Tool

Determine if a database will help your learners acquire the rules of your lesson. Are there more than two rules/principles to be learned? Are they related rules that might have steps or applications confused with one another? If the answer to these questions is yes, a database could be helpful.

Determine if you want to show students a database or have them construct their own. If you want the database to function as a help or review aid, you probably want to construct one yourself. If you want the database to function as a learning strategy aid or practice exercise, students should construct their own:

```
Rule: Salami Principle

Steps: 1. Identify task
       2. Slice into manageable bites.
       3. Estimate time of each bite.
       4. Complete one bite at a time.

Example:Organizing a meeting can be sliced
into 1. Soliciting participants (1 hr.),
2. Agreeing on a time/date (1 hr.),
3. Setting an agenda (2 hours),4. Securing
facilities, (1/2 hour), Disseminating
notices (1/2 hour).

Used With: Means-End Analysis

Subskills: Task identification
           Task prioritization
```

```
       Complete the Following Rule:

Rule: Salami Principle

Steps: 1. _____
       2. _____
       3. _____
       4. _____

(Type in an example): _____
_____
_____.

Used With: _____

Subskills: _____
           _____
```

The first example is a database shown to students, the second is one that students construct. In a given lesson, both database strategies can be used. Students can be given the database, and then construct their own.

Decide how to use the database in the lesson. If students are shown the database, it can be used as a help or review segment. If they are to construct one, it can be used as a practice exercise at different points in the lesson, or as a final practice:

```
     The next principle we will discuss
  is the Distraction Avoidance principle.


        Press "R" to review rules

        Press RETURN to go on
```

```
     The next principle we will look
  at is Distraction Avoidance.


     Before we do, let's see if you
  can summarize the three rules
  you've seen so far.

  RETURN to make a database.
```

In the first example, students study a given database, in the second they construct one. Either strategy can help students learn to solve problems with rules. However, neither of these takes the place of having students *solve* problems using rules. They still must apply the rules to learn them, even when they do construct a database.

When using the database as a help or reference tool, it can be programmed for students to browse through specific fields of information across all the separate rule records. For example, students can search the field "applications" across all rule records:

```
  To review time management principles,
  select what you would like to see:

     1. rule steps
     2. rule applications
     3. all data on each rule

  Enter the number of your choice and
   press RETURN.
```

This "field search" allows students to reference specific information quickly. It becomes more useful as the database becomes larger.

Consider adding some of the following options to your database to improve its effectiveness:

If you give students a rule database, have them rearrange the information into new fields or records, or have them add onto a database you have already given them. This encourages active processing of rule information.

If students are making a database, have them complete one single field for each rule record, and then complete another field. For example, they could do the "steps" field first, and then the "examples" field. This strategy makes students compare all the rules each time they complete a field.

If students are constructing or adding onto a database, set the computer to record and store their input. You can then print out their database responses and evaluate them.

You Do It: Construct a Rule Database

If the number and type of lesson rules make a database appropriate, construct a database tool or exercise for students:

Screen Sequence 1 (displays of database information given by you):

Screen Sequence 2 (students practice making or using databases):

Screen Sequence 3 (screens that tell or guide students to use the database. This may require rewriting previous lesson screens to include a review or help command to reference the database, or creating new screens that announce a database construction exercise to students):

Evaluating Rule Tutorials

Most of the CAI software created and used by teachers is tutorial, as opposed to simulations, games, etc. Therefore, we have included a brief section on how to evaluate CAI tutorial programs.

When completing a rule tutorial, review the final lesson using the checklist outlined below. This checklist can be used as an evaluation tool for commercially made software as well.

When evaluating commercial software, the first question to ask is "Does the lesson teach rule learning outcomes?" This cannot be judged by reading the program title or its instructions, even if it says that it is a rule learning lesson: it can only be done by trying out the program itself, to see if it actually teaches the solution of problems based on applications of clearly defined rules. Sometimes, a purported rule lesson will actually teach problem solving, or verbal information.

Evaluation Checklist
(Answer each question by checking one of three categories:)

	None	Adequate	Very Good
1. Requires rule application?			
2. Readiness activities provided?			
3. Sub-steps outlined?			
4. Examples of application provided?			
5. Examples explained?			
6. Practice provided?			
7. Diagnostic feedback?			
8. Branching and help?			

When evaluating either your own program or commercial software, it is critical that you find several sample students and have them try out the program. Sit down next to the students and watch them use the program. Take notes on their comments and behavior. If it is a program you created, make corrections in the program, and try it again with another student. This can be done when the program is coded into the computer or when it is still on paper. Either way, this will help you discover any problems with the lesson before using it for instruction.

Summary

Rule learning involves the application of a specific principle or procedure to solve specific problems. All effective rule learning lessons have a certain set of lesson components, whether they are taught on the computer or not. In particular, rules must involve understanding the steps involved in applying a rule, and practice in applying these rules to solve problems. Computer tutorials, deductive and inductive, are the most effective methods for learning rules on the computer, and include practice and feedback segments. To develop and enhance rules that are learned, there are a variety of applications strategies: games, simulations, and drills. There are also various problem solving tools that can help in the application of rules to problems.

Chapter 6

Programming a CAI Lesson
for Problem Solving Learning

Characteristics of Problem Solving
Behavior and Learning

Overview

Problem solving involves the creative use of rules and concepts to solve complex problems. Compared to rule using behavior, problem solving requires more creative or originative thinking on the part of the learner. In rule using, the learner must apply a given rule to a specific type of problem. In problem solving, the learner must frequently invent the method for solving the problem. Problem solving is a complex intellectual skill. Any given problem may be soluble by more than one acceptable method, and there may be more than one acceptable solution as well. Consequently, designing CAI instruction for problem solving can be very challenging.

Definition

Problem solving is a learned method or approach used to solve a wide variety of problems. In many cases, a correct solution can take a variety of forms. The method does involve the utilization of concepts and rules to solve problems, but it usually does not have the specific, step-by-step procedures of rule using. Rather, it involves the selective and creative application of combinations of rules/principles by the problem solver.

A problem solving method is often described by general principles or steps used in solving the problem. A general step may be "define the problem" or "list all problem variables." A general principle may be "all correct solutions have only one unknown variable" or "hypotheses must be verifiable." In any case, the method is applicable to a broader range of problems than rule using, and is usually broader in definition than most rule procedures.

Rules and problem solving outcomes are very similar to one another, in that they both solve problems. One difference is the specificity of the problems and procedures; rules are used when the problem requires mere application of a previously learned procedure or method. When the problem requires the adaptation of old methods or the creation of new ones, problem solving outcomes are involved.

Problem Solving Behaviors

A person has learned problem solving when he or she can:

Generate the solution to a complex math word problem.

Compose an original story about his or her summer vacation.

Choose "the best" presidential candidate.

Utilize Spanish grammar rules to conduct a conversation.

Negotiate an agreement between disputing parties.

Design a computer lesson.

Create a poem.

Critique a business report.

Learned Behaviors That Are
Not Problem Solving

Solving long division problems (rule using).

Determining the type of problem to be solved (concept learning).

Describing how to go about solving a problem (this is verbal information, although figuring out how to do it would be problem solving).

Self-Check on Problem Solving

1. Think of some examples of problem solving:

    Can you think of some that are part of your job?

    Can you think of some general methods or approaches you use with a wide variety of problems?

    Can you think of cases where there is more than one correct colution, no one way to solve the problem?

2. Check to make sure that the examples are problem solving:

    Does the problem require creative use of rules or principles, not following a set of specific steps?

    Can the solution method only be described in general terms, if at all?

3. Check your lesson objective sub-objectives from the lesson map you completed in part 1: Are you really teaching problem solving? If students simply recite the method for solving a problem, you are teaching verbal information. If the method is more of a "recipe" or procedure approach to a set of specific problems, you are probably teaching rule learning. These outcomes are described in chapter 3 and 5.

Problem Solving Learning

A person has learned problem solving when he or she can utilize previously learned knowledge and skills to creatively solve a problem. This often involves using concepts and rules. In some cases, the problem solver learns a general method that can be creatively applied to a variety of problems. An example is the scientific method. In other cases, it may be difficult or impossible to describe even a general solution procedure. In these cases, learners acquire a set of general guidelines or *benchmarks*, such as guidelines for writing poetry, which tell them if their attempts are "on the right track." Creative, originative, evaluative, and adaptive behaviors are signs of problem solving outcomes.

Of all types of learning outcomes, problem solving may be the most difficult to teach and learn. It is difficult to teach because it is difficult for the teacher to specify the problem solving process, and to evaluate student solutions and pinpoint difficulties. It is difficult to learn because it may take a sizable amount of time to acquire the skills, time to learn and practice the process.

Lesson Components for Problem Solving Learning

Overview

Most problem solving lessons should contain the following components:

the objective of the lesson

a description of the problem solving process

an example of an application of the process or its sub-steps

explanations of how the process was applied

characteristics of good and bad solutions

benchmarks to measure problem solving progress

practice problems that require a solution through use of the process and its sub-steps

feedback that allows students to judge the merit of their solutions

learning strategies that facilitate problem solving learning

These lesson components assume that the student has not previously learned the problem solving method, although he or she may have learned component concepts and rules. Students are given a computer tutorial that teaches them all of the preceding lesson components. If the student has already mastered or used the problem solving method, a non-tutorial strategy may be used, such as a drill, game, or simulation. These non-tutorial strategies are used to enhance the student's problem solving skills through varied practice. Both tutorial and non-tutorial strategies are outlined in this chapter.

The lesson components may be sequenced differently in different lessons, depending on the teaching strategy used and the problem solving method taught. In some cases, you may *present* the problem solving process to the student, which is a deductive tutorial strategy. In other cases, you may have the student *infer* the problem solving process, based on personal experience. This is more of an inductive strategy. Where the student has already learned the process, you may use a practice and feedback sequence such as a game or drill.

In this chapter we describe and exemplify the important components of a problem solving lesson.

Objectives

*Why Do It: The Effectiveness of
CAI Lesson Objectives*

Introducing the lesson is an important part of problem solving instruction. As learning research has indicated, the introductory part of the lesson can be used to help the student recall previous learning that is relevant to the new lesson content, and mentally prepare the student for the type of learning that is to take place.

One of the best ways to introduce a problem solving lesson is to explain the objective of the lesson. This is especially important in problem solving instruction, since the outcome may be difficult to learn, and students may not know what is expected of them. By knowing the objective of the lesson first, the student can organize subsequent problem solving instruction around the stated objective, thus increasing the probability of mastering that objective.

In addition, understanding the objective of the lesson can reduce anxiety in learners, since they understand the purposes of the computer lesson. Problem solving instruction can be particularly complex and open-ended (as compared to concept or rule instruction). Frequently, learners find that there are neither simple specific processes to learn, nor clear-cut correct solutions. As a result, there is a greater likelihood of performance anxiety by the learner; hence the utility of stating the objective.

*How to Do It: Presenting
Lesson Objectives*

Informing the learner of the objective. When writing an effective problem solving objective, be as accurate as possible in the description of the objective. Avoid statements of content ("this lesson is about the scientific method"). Instead, describe what the students will be able to do when they have completed the lesson. When students learn problem solving skills, they usually learn to originate or generate solutions for a wide range of problems.

```
In this lesson you will learn

to originate your own method for

conducting an empirical test to

solve a research problem,

using the scientific method.
```

```
After completing this lesson

on haiku poetry, you will be

able to write your own haikus

on a given subject.
```

For difficult topics, you can also explain that the lesson will require a lot of thought or practice. In other words, prepare the student for any difficulties that may lie ahead.

Presenting lesson sub-objectives. In addition to the main objective, the objectives statement can include the sub-objectives of the problem solving lesson. These can be the sub-steps of the problem solving process, or the rules and concepts that the student uses in solving the problem:

```
To design your empirical test,

you will learn how to do the

following test activities:

  o explain the research problem

  o generate alternative solutions

  o design test procedures and methods
```

These sub-objectives can be listed along with the major objective in the lesson introduction. Statements of sub-objectives are clearer to the learner when a moderate number of them (five or fewer) are listed, as opposed to a long list of sub-objectives.

You Do It: Define the Objectives and Sub-objectives

1. Write down the major objective of your problem solving lesson, as you want the students to see it on the computer:

    _____

    _____

2. You can also include a statement or list of the sub-steps of the problem solving method (if any) which are used to master the objective. These sub-objectives should reflect the lesson sub-outcomes that you outlined in part 1.

    _____

    _____

Self-Check on Objective(s)

Does your objective use a problem solving verb (create, evaluate, invent, etc.)?

Does your objective state the context or subject for application of the problem solving method (*what* will be solved)?

If you listed sub-objectives, are they skills that must be learned in order to master the main objective?

Presenting the Lesson Purpose

Why Do It: Motivating the
Student to Persevere

More than any other kind of learning outcomes, problem solving requires student perseverance and motivation to learn, since the outcome is not easily learned. When students know the value or function of what they learn, it tends to increase their will to learn. This motivational effect is particularly prevalent with adult and young adult students.

How to Do It: Composing a Statement
of Purpose of Function

An explanation of the purpose or function of learning the lesson objective can be included in the introduction to the lesson. If an explanation is used, it can follow the objectives/sub-objectives statement, on a separate computer screen. The explanation can tell students how they can use the problem solving outcome when they are done.

```
Once you have learned to use
the scientific method correctly,
you can design laboratory experiments
that are both theoretically and
methodologically sound.
```

```
Writers who learn to compose
haikus find that they take
a fresh approach to all their
writing. They learn to express
their thoughts differently.
```

As in the haiku example, the statement can indicate that the problem solving skill can transfer to other problem solving situations (writing prose, for example).

You Do It: State the Lesson Purpose

1. Write down the purpose of your lesson, as you want the students to see it on the computer:

   _____

   _____

Self-Check on Lesson Purpose

Have you explained the benefits of learning problem solving, how it can be used to the reader's benefit?

Is your description sincere and believable, or does it sound as if you are trying to "sell" the lesson?

Describing the Problem Solving Process

Why Do It: The Importance of a Process Description

Problem solving learning can be more difficult to teach than any other type of learning. This is because it can be very difficult to describe the problem solving process. In some cases, the instructor may not be able to tell students *how* they can go about solving problems, but can only describe the general procedures for solution, or just the general characteristics of a correct or incorrect solution.

In general, the best way to teach students problem solving is to (1) describe the steps of the problem solving process, (2) present examples of the application of these steps to problems, and (3) provide cues or benchmarks that students can use to assess their approach to solving the problem. The purpose of these instructional methods is to give students a chance to mentally formulate their own general problem solving model, one that contains both procedures and criteria for solutions, as well as examples for future reference. All that then remains is to familiarize students with the idea that problem solving is not a lock-step (rule using) process, thus developing in students the proper problem solving attitudes of persistence and inventiveness.

How to Do It: Presenting Information
and Learning Guidance

Developing instruction on problem solving involves four basic instructional activities:

1. Eliciting students' recall of previously learned skills and knowledge relevant to problem solving.

2. Describing the problem solving process, including the sub-steps of the process.

3. Describing the general characteristics of acceptable or unacceptable solutions to problems.

4. Presenting example application(s) of the process and/or its sub-steps to the solution of a problem.

These steps are described below.

Eliciting recall of prior knowledge. You may have accomplished the first step, eliciting recall of prior knowledge and skills, when you completed part 1 of the workbook (preparing the learner for new instruction). However, if you have not developed a lesson segment that requires the learner to review skills or information that they have already learned, you should do so now. Since problem solving is a complex skill, there is often prior knowledge and a number of prerequisite skills that the learner must have meastered before beginning the lesson.

To elicit recall of previous learning, either tell the students about it or have students answer questions about what they have learned:

```
In the last lesson on experimentation,
you learned the five basic steps of
the scientific method, which involved
defining the problem, formulating and
selecting hypotheses, and testing a
selected hypothesis.

Press RETURN to continue lesson . . .
```

```
The previous lesson had
the basic steps of the
scientific method. Do
you recall the first two?

a) awareness & definition
b) hypothesis & testing
c) definition & hypothesis

Choose a letter & RETURN
```

Note that in the second example, the student is given a review question that must be answered. Review exercises and quizzes are useful ways of eliciting recall of prior knowledge, because they force the learner to think about the topic in order to respond to the question.

Describing the process. In describing the problem solving process to students, the crucial question is "Does the process have any major sub-steps that can be described?" If so, the CAI lesson should present an overview coupled with a description for each sub-step:

Overview

```
The application of the scientific method
to experiments means that experiments must
be designed and conducted to select and
test the most viable hypothesis. To design
such an experiment, the experimenter must:

1. Define the research problem.

2. Describe alternative hypotheses to the
   solution of that problem.

3. Select and justify a given experimental
   hypothesis.

4. Describe and justify the experimental
   methods used to verify the hypothesis.
```

Description of a sub-step

```
Defining the research problem (step 1)
involves stating the problem in clear
and simple terms.

More important, the history of research
on the problem has to be summarized, as
well as the significance of the problem.
```

Note that these sub-steps are more general than the sub-steps of a rule, and in fact are *each* a general rule. Using them together makes this a problem solving activity.

If the problem solving process has more than three sub-steps, and these are fairly complex, it is possible to take each of the sub-steps as a separate lesson, with the overview of the entire problem solving process as a type of introduction to the series of lessons. Practice and instruction on how to solve problems by combining the sub-steps would be provided at the end of the series.

Describing general solution characteristics. In some cases, the problem solving method being taught does not have a set of specific steps that can be described. In such cases, the instructor may want to describe the general conditions or characteristics of solutions to the problem. These conditions can include the general characteristics of an acceptable solution:

Description of solution characteristics

```
A good haiku poem has 17 syllables,
written in 3 lines, with a 5-7-5
syllable arrangement. Each haiku
expresses a single idea that evokes
an emotional response in the reader.

          (GRAPHIC)

In this lesson, we will look at each
of these requirements in turn.
```

Presenting problem solving examples. After the general problem solving process sub-steps or conditions have been described, the student should see some examples of the application of the problem solving process. This can be difficult to do on a computer, since the application examples may be too wordy or lengthy to fit onto a computer screen.

If examples of problem solving application are rather complex, the instructor has several options to remedy this problem:

Present a simplified example of the entire problem.

Present sections of the problem example in sequence.

Present the application examples off-screen.

Several of these options can be used together, such as presenting a simplified example off-screen:

Presenting a simplified and partial example

```
A statement of the research problem
should take the form:

"Studies/theories x, y, and z have
explored this problem in previous
work, but have not (obtained conclusive
results)/(focused on this aspect of
the problem)."
```

Presenting an off-screen example

```
To see how an experiment should be
defined and outlined, look at Case
Study 1, in the green notebook. Note
that each aspect of the research model
has been circled and identified
in this study.

Press RETURN when you are done with
the study . . .
```

After a simple or partial example of problem solution is given to the student, the next step is to give the student a more complete or complex example of the problem. If possible, the subject matter of this second example should be somewhat different from that of the first example shown to the student. This helps the student learn to generalize the problem solving method to a variety of problems.

In each of the problem examples given, the instructor has the option of also indicating the characteristics of an acceptable solution to the problem. These can be characteristics of the final solution to the problem or of a sub-step solution to a complex problem. These characteristics serve as benchmarks or criteria that students can use to gauge the progress of their own attempts to solve problems given them. For lengthy/complex problems, they can use benchmarks to evaluate each stage (sub-step) of their solution.

Benchmark for a sub-step

```
Note that the "Research Method" also
describes the research subjects
and their characteristics relevant to the
research problem.

It also outlines each step of the
experiment, in chronological order.
```

After several problem examples have been presented to the student, the next step is to provide the student with some problem solving practice. Practice is the subject of the next section of this book.

*You Do It: Compose a Description of
the Problem Solving Process*

Write out a description of the problem solving process the student will learn, complete with examples of problem solutions. Remember that the instruction can embody a variety of strategies:

Eliciting recall of prior relevant knowledge.

Describing the problem solving process.
    describing sub-steps of the process
    describing problem solving conditions

Presenting examples of problem solutions.
    simplified versions
    partial versions
    on-screen or off-screen versions
    benchmarks for self-evaluation

The exact combination of problem solving strategies you choose should be based on the content of your lesson and the complexity of the problem solving process being taught. Your selected strategies should correspond to teaching strategies you would use if you were individually tutoring a student in problem solving.

Write out each problem solving description and example on a separate sheet of regular 8½-by-11-inch paper. Compose each sheet as it will appear to the student on the computer screen. Use a separate sheet of paper for each screen. Remember that the computer screen is smaller than a sheet of paper, and some space should be left at the bottom of each "screen" for keyboard directions such as "Hit RETURN to go to the next frame."

Screen Sequence 1 (recall of prior knowledge):

Screen Sequence 2 (description of process):

Screen Sequence 3 (examples of process):

Screen Sequence 4 (benchmarks/solution characteristics):

Self-Check on Problem Description

Have you designed the program to recall all of the sub-skills and knowledge required to learn the problem solving method?

Is the problem solving process described in terminology that all your students will understand? Is it complete?

Have all sub-steps to the process been clearly indicated?

(If you are describing solution characteristics). Have you included essential characteristics of good solutions? Are there any common characteristics of incorrect solutions that you should include?

Designing Practice for Problem Solving

*Why Do It: The Importance of
Problem Solving Practice*

As with other intellectual skills, students can only learn problem solving by applying their skills to problem solving exercises. Since problem solving can be the most difficult intellectual skill to master, the provision for student practice in instruction becomes crucial. Through repeated practice, the student learns to creatively apply previously learned rules and concepts to the solution of complex and openended problems. Through practice with a variety of problems, the student learns to apply these skills across different types of problems, ensuring that his or her problem solving skills will generalize to a variety of situations.

*How to Do It: Designing the Sequence
and Variety of Exercises*

To teach problem solving, the teacher should design several varied problem solving exercises. The difficulty is that problem solving exercises can be complex, and may not easily fit onto a computer screen. Thus, the CAI author should design student problem solving practice in the following manner:

1. Compose several problem solving exercises on paper. Present easy exercises first, with more difficult ones following. Vary the subject matter in the exercises.

2. Determine if the exercises can be adapted to the computer; that they will fit onto the screen in a logical fashion.

3. If the exercises are not adaptable, design on-screen instruction that prompts students to utilize the off-screen exercises.

4. Design the feedback for the exercises.

This sequence assumes that lesson authors should first determine the best type of problem solving exercise and then judge its appropriateness for the computer, instead of first determining what will fit onto the computer and making that their problem solving exercise. In other words, instruction determines computer characteristics; computer characteristics do not determine instruction.

Composing problem solving exercises. Generally, the first exercise each student encounters should be relatively easy, with harder ones following. Even if students will do only one or two problems for practice, a simplified or partial practice problem can serve as a useful introduction to practice. This easy-to-hard sequence allows students to initially focus on applying their problem solving skills to a simple problem instead of trying to understand a complex one.

To design an easy exercise for the initial practice item, the CAI author can (1) Use a version of the problem familiar to the student, one similar (not identical) to problem examples you have already presented; (2) Furnish a simplified version of the problem, with some of the problem detail/complexity missing; or (3) Ask the student to solve several parts of the overall problem, one part at a time. Make sure that all exercises reflect the lesson's problem solving objective: that the student must in some way originate or generate a solution to a problem.

Partial and simplified version of a problem

```
Let's see if you can design an
experiment using the scientific
method. You will need to describe
the hypothesis, procedures, and
measurement instruments that you
would use for the following experiment:

To determine if 6-year-olds know how to
correctly operate a soda vending machine.

 Enter your version of the hypothesis:

 _____

 _____
```

In the preceding example, a simple research problem is used, and the student only has to use the "formulate the hypothesis" stage of the overall method.

As you design subsequent exercises, make sure that the subject matter and/or complexity changes from the simple initial problem. If a student's initial exercise involved writing a story about his or her summer vacation, the next exercise could involve writing about the student's family, as a change of subject matter. If a student is learning to design laboratory experiments, subsequent exercises should differ in experimental subjects and procedures.

Determining the adaptability of exercises to CAI. There are two problems in designing CAI exercises for problem solving: (1) the problem may be too lengthy to fit onto a computer screen, and (2) the student's answers may be too complex or lengthy for the computer to easily evaluate. If either of these problems occurs, the teacher may decide to have the student practice the problem off-screen.

If the problem exercise description is too long for the screen, the computer can direct the student to solve the problem off-screen:

```
Now let's try our hand at using the
scientific method.  You should have a
green binder that says "Lesson 1 Exercises."

Open the binder to page 1, and do the first
exercise.

After you have completed the exercise, press
CONTROL-R for some feedback about a correct
answer to this problem.
```

You can also provide off-screen practice and feedback, or a booklet can be used to provide practice answers, instead of the computer.

The range of possible student answers is also an important consideration in designing on-screen or off-screen exercises. Quite often, the correct answers to a single problem may be so complex and varied that it is difficult to tell the computer what answers to accept as right. For example, if a student has to compose a poem or design a city bus plan, the answer may be better judged by the instructor than the computer. In such cases, the student can be directed to produce the answer off-screen for evaluation.

Designing Feedback for Problem Exercises

Why Do It: The Effect of Feedback
on Problem Solving Learning

"Feedback" is the knowledge of results that a student receives about practice performance. The computer "feeds back" a message to students about what they did and why it is right or wrong. Properly designed feedback messages allow students to correct any errors in their performance and affirm to themselves what they are doing right. Until students know that they are right, or how they are wrong, the learning they derive from practice is incomplete. Thus, the design of feedback can be just as important as the design of practice exercises.

Feedback is particularly important for problem solving, owing to the nature of the practice exercises. For complex or time consuming problems, feedback can be used to correct student mistakes *before* the problem is completed. For creative problems that may have more than one acceptable answer (writing a poem, critiquing a formula), well-designed feedback helps students to evaluate *their own* responses. In problem solving, the range of correct answers is less obvious than in other learning outcomes. Thus, feedback becomes more necessary to the student, but more difficult to design.

How to Do It: Designing Individualized
Feedback Messages

Feedback is more than a message that simply tells students they are right or wrong. Especially for problem solving, good feedback tells students *how* they were wrong or *why* they were wrong (the type of mistake); even why they were right. Feedback can be provided for students who feel they do not even know enough to try to answer the practice given them (this is called a help section). In addition, different feedback messages or routines can be given to students who are on their second or third try at a practice exercise.

The computer is a useful medium for conveying feedback, because it can display different feedback messages for different types of right and wrong answers. Also, the computer can send students back to an exercise that they have missed, and count the number of times a student tries it. It can even send a struggling student to a remedial or HELP module, to provide some additional instruction, and then send the student right back to the practice exercises. This ability to send students to previous exercises or new instructional sections is called the *branching* capability of the computer. It can be combined with feedback messages to produce a variety of computer responses for various students' practice performances.

For problem solving instruction, the design of feedback is especially challenging, for several reasons. First, many problems involve students generating or creating their own answers. For these outcomes, multiple-choice answer formats are frequently inapplicable, thus eliminating a simple answer judging format for feedback. Second, the variety and complexity of answers can make it difficult for the computer to assess the correctness of student responses. Third, the feedback message you want to give the student may be too lengthy to fit onto a single computer screen.

The types of feedback you design will depend in part on the types of problem solving exercises you have planned. Are the students given a simplified version of the problem as an initial exercise? Are they given a sequence of parts of a problem, or the entire problem? Is their answer to be given on-screen or off-screen? Can you give a single correct solution to the exercise as feedback to the student, or are only the characteristics of a good solution given? If the student is wrong, will he or she have time to make a second try at the problem? There are a number of considerations to designing feedback for problem solving—so many, that feedback design is a complex problem solving activity itself.

Note: if your problem solving exercises have definite and specific correct answers (such as "this patient has scoliosis," or "3x + 10y = 18"), go to the feedback section of chapter 5. Chapter 5 describes feedback options for specific answers. For non-specific answers, read the procedures outlined next.

If the answers to your practice problems will be variable and open-ended responses, consider following the procedures below:

1. Review the problem solving exercises you have designed, to determine if you can give either a prototype answer as a solution or the general characteristics of a good/bad solution as feedback. This feedback can be given for individual parts of a problem as well as the problem as a whole.

2. Decide if the feedback will be on-screen or off-screen, based on the complexity and length of the feedback message. If off-screen, decide if it will be delivered by instructor, text, media, or other students.

3. (For on-screen feedback) decide if the student will be given a second or third chance at the problem, and if you want to design any HELP or remedial sequences for the student to access.

4. Compose all feedback messages, including branching, HELP, or remedial frames.

5. Do a dry run through the exercises and feedback messages. Read and respond as a student would, and try all combinations of right/wrong answers and number of tries that you can anticipate.

Problem solutions and solution characteristics as feedback. Where there is more than one answer to the problem exercise, give a prototype or model version of the correct answer:

```
Your answer to the research hypothesis
problem should be something like this:

"The hypothesis is that there would be
no significant differences in concept
identification tasks between children
that were exposed to adjunct tutoring
and those children that were not."

Compare your answer to this one.

 Press RETURN to go on, or CTRL-R for
 more practice.
```

Similar to the benchmarks used for problem solving guidance, the model solutions are used for student self-evaluation and guidance. This method can best be used when you anticipate that all correct responses will be some variation of this type of answer. In such cases, the computer does not "judge" the student's answer, but provides an example for the student to use in evaluation of his or her own response.

Where the variety of student responses may be too great for a prototype example, you can specify the criteria or characteristics of an acceptable solution as student feedback, or even the characteristics of an unacceptable solution. Whether acceptable or unacceptable solution characteristics are used depends on your own certainty that all good or bad solutions have these respective characteristics. In other words, you have to be sure that at least all good solutions have characteristics x,y,z, or all bad solutions are a,b,c:

```
Your research methodology for the concept
learning hypothesis should have included
all of the following:

    1.   Two dependent variables

    2.   At least three experimental groups

    3.   Some measure of long-term retention

If your methodology did not include these
three elements, press RETURN for another
problem.  If it did, press ESCAPE for a
new lesson.
```

Note that in this example, students are given a choice of lesson segments to move to, depending on their evaluations of their answer. They branch themselves instead of the computer doing it.

Designing off-screen and on-screen feedback. On-screen feedback can be used for all on-screen exercises. However, it can also be used for off-screen exercises (such as paper and pencil work) that the computer assigns students to complete as practice. Students work the problem off-screen and receive feedback on the screen. This is possible because the computer does not judge the student's answer, but instead provides a solution or solution characteristics for students to use in evaluating their own responses.

However, if the feedback can only be given off-screen (due to its length or complexity), the computer can be used to direct the student to the proper feedback source. The off-screen feedback medium can be text, media, students, or live instructor.

```
Describe the hypothesis, procedures,
and measurements that you would use
for the following experiment:


To determine if 6-year-olds know how to
correctly operate a soda vending machine.


Take a sheet of paper and write out each
one of the method's experimental steps.

When you have completed the problem,
take it to your instructor for evaluation.


After your instructor has evaluated the
problem, press TAB to continue.
```

```
Now that you have written your haiku
about Winter, check your poem against
those on pages 90 & 91 of the text
Popular Haikus on the Seasons.

Check your poem's structure against
the examples. Is your poem as figurative
as theirs, or more literal?
```

In each of the preceding examples, the computer directs the student to use an off-screen source for feedback, in one case an instructor, in another a book.

Designing help and remedial sequences. Since the student may run into difficulties when solving problems, you may choose to incorporate some help for the student. This can take the form of supplementary instruction, cues or hints, or a review of previous instruction.

In CAI, help or remediation is frequently given to the student automatically by the computer, after the computer has judged that the student made errors on the exercises given. However, in problem solving exercises the correct answers may be too varied for a computer to assess student responses. Thus, the CAI lesson may be designed to allow students to *choose* their remediation or help, instead of the computer giving it. The choice for this type of feedback can be built into the problem exercise frame:

```
Let's see if you can design an experiment
via the scientific method. You will need
to describe the hypothesis, procedures,
and measurements that you would use for
the following experiment:

To determine if 6-year-olds know how to
correctly operate a soda vending machine.

Enter your version of the hypothesis:

_____


        Press R to review the lesson . . .
        Press H for a hint . . .
```

Of course, the computer can also direct students to seek off-screen help (i.e., the teacher) if they are having difficulty solving the problem.

*You Do It: Compose Practice
and Feedback Frames*

Design the practice and feedback frames for the problem solving lesson. This can include any branching or help-remediation sequences that you may want to develop for the student.

Composing the practice frames. Take a sheet of paper and compose each practice exercise that the student will do. Give consideration to the following:

Using a simplified or easy problem at the outset.

Varying the content of different problem exercises.

Using student response formats that faithfully reflect the objective of your lesson; ones that require students to originate or generate their own answers.

(For complex exercises) using parts of the problem process as separate exercises, or using off-screen exercises.

Screen Sequence 1 (simple or partial problem screens):

Screen Sequence 2 (harder problem or next part of a problem):

Self-Check on Practice Frames

Do each of your practice frames require a problem solving behavior, where the student works toward all or part of a solution?

Have cues or help been provided for each exercise frame?

Have you started with simpler problems first?

Have you been able to adequately present the problems on-screen, or would off-screen practice be better?

Composing the feedback frames. For each of the exercise frames written, take a sheet of paper and draw a vertical line down the middle of the page:

1. On one side of the paper, write down all the acceptable solutions to the problem, or ideal/prototypical correct solutions, or the characteristics of a correct solution.

2. On the other side of the paper, list all types of feedback messages the student will receive, including off-screen directions, solution characteristics, and (on another sheet if needed) remediation/help instruction. In particular, consider feedback that describes the characteristics or criteria of acceptable/unacceptable solutions.

3. If students are to be branched back to previous lessons or to other parts, you should describe their destinations. For example, if they are sent back·to an earlier part of the lesson, you could write something like "if answer wrong on first try, go back to beginning of Lesson 1." This is navigational information to remind you where the feedback frame will show up. It is not seen by the student, but it is used by the programmer.

Screen Sequence 1 (solutions on one side of paper):

Screen Sequence 2 (feedback messages on other side of paper):

Self-Check on Feedback for Practice

Have you avoided the temptation to give students the answer when they are wrong, and instead provide cues or help?

Where solutions are unspecifiable, do your cues indicate necessary characteristics of good solutions?

If you have on-screen feedback, could it be better delivered off-screen? Would the students then receive more complete help?

Have you included feedback for all types of anticipated student responses, including unanticipated or "totally lost" ones?

Learning Strategies to Facilitate Problem Solving

Why Do It: Facilitating Problem Solving

As you have seen from the previous sections of this chapter, problem solving is the most complex type of learning. Problem solving may require:

identification and selection of relevant information from the environment;

selection of appropriate rules, concepts, and principles;

extrapolation of inferences from the information;

synthesis of those rules, etc., into a plan;

application of that plan;

evaluation of that plan; and

drawing of conclusions, inferences, and implications from the results.

These are complex thinking processes that students do not normally do. Therefore, the students need help in developing these skills. Otherwise, they may try using ineffective strategies to solve problems.

As we have pointed out in previous chapters, CAI often requires inclusion of learning strategies that facilitate the development of those skills. Problem solving learning strategies not only help the learners to solve problems, but also how to *learn* how to solve problems. Problem solving learning strategies provide students with generalizable problem solving skills. These learning strategies differ from practice and feedback sequences.

Elaboration strategies are an important set of learning strategies for problem solving. Elaboration strategies require the learner to elaborate upon information by adding personal meaning to the information. For example, generating mental images or creating mental maps makes new information more meaningful for learners.

The complexity of the problem solving process requires that some of the learning strategies important to facilitating problem solving skills are *meta-learning*. Meta-learning strategies help learners to become aware of their own learning behavior, and monitor learning progress. Students are not simply using a strategy, but rather observing their use of the strategy and evaluating how effectively it is working. *Meta* means "after" or "used with to form a new." Meta-learning normally occurs after learning when the student monitors his or her learning. Meta-learning also refers to the critical analysis of one's learning progress. Students who are skilled in meta-learning strategies consciously select strategies for learning, and monitor their effectiveness in using them. When they are ineffective, students try another strategy. Meta-learning strategies are important for complex thinking processes such as problem solving.

How to Do It: Embedding Problem Solving
Learning Strategies in CAI

Two types of elaboration strategies, both similar, might be used to facilitate components of the problem solving process. These strategies are inferencing and implication/hypothesis forming.

Inferencing strategy. Problem solving requires that learners identify, select, and apply relevant rules. Asking learners to infer causes of events or conditions at different points of the problem solving process requires them to select the operative rule and to decide how it applies in a particular situation. These types of questions would most effectively be embedded in the examples or practice questions to guide learners through the process.

```
Why do you think that
studies X, Y and Z obtained
inconclusive results?

Hint: What information was
not included in the report?
```

Inference questions ask why, rather than which or what. They also ask students for their own opinions, instead of giving them as feedback.

Implication/hypothesis strategy. Similar to the inferencing strategy, the implication/hypothesis strategy asks students for their opinions. But rather than asking why something happened, students are asked to predict or extrapolate from existing information. This is also known as a hypothesis strategy, because hypotheses are statements of implication.

```
We know, from reading Case Study 1,
that most 6-year-olds like sodas.
------------------------------------
What implications can we draw?

What can we predict about the
likelihood that they can operate
soda machines?
```

It is important in solving problems that students be willing to make predictions from information that they encounter. The more often students are called upon to do that, the more generalizable that skill becomes.

Meta-learning strategies. As indicated above, meta-learning strategies are those in which learners analyze and evaluate their own learning. Two specific meta-learning strategies are helping learners plan their learning through CAI, and helping learners evaluate their learning.

Estimating task difficulty. A major reason students fail to learn is that they have not committed the necessary time and effort to the process. This is especially significant with problem solving, because of its complexity. Estimating task difficulty consists of a variety of activities that may help the learners gauge the amount of effort necessary for solving problems. You might provide the new information to be encountered in the lesson, with an estimation of the difficulty to learn it:

```
In this lesson, you will have to:

  Define the research problem
  Develop hypotheses
  Select the experimental hypotheses
  Select experimental methods

This information should all be new to
you, so this lesson might be
difficult.
```

The instructor might alternatively present the important rules or concepts and ask the learners to evaluate their knowledge of each. If their level of familiarity is high, task difficulty should be minimal. Communicate that to the learners.

Evaluating comprehension. After students have completed the lesson, or during any phase of the lesson, the instructor should stimulate them to evaluate their understanding of the material. This might be a simple question, such as "Did you understand the text that you just read?" or "Did that example clearly illustrate the components of a haiku?" Another approach would be:

```
Which topics were unclear?

List them below:

_____

_____
```

```
Are there parts of the
presentation that you
would like to reread?

_____

_____
```

This type of question can be embedded frequently throughout the lesson, at different stages of problem solving. It is an important strategy. Getting learners used to evaluating their understanding is important. During the early phases of this strategy, you might want to provide some advice about the learner's performance. That is, if performance on practice items is inadequate but a student never indicates any comprehension problems, then you may want to recommend more intense scrutiny of that student's understanding.

You Do It: Compose Strategies to
Facilitate Problem Solving

Write out a description of some learning strategies that would facilitate problem solving. Remember, these strategies can be:

Elaboration

Inferring causes or problems from events or situations

Stating implications of conditions or information and generating hypotheses from information

Meta-learning

Estimating the difficulty of learning a task

Evaluating comprehension or understanding of information

The exact strategies that you use will depend upon the complexity of the problem being taught. Which strategies will facilitate that problem solution and where in the instruction should they go?

Using a sheet of paper, design the learning strategy activity as it will appear on the screen. Do not forget to leave room for directions and navigational information.

Screen Sequence 1 (elaboration strategy or strategies):

Screen Sequence 2 (evaluating strategy or strategies):

Self-Check on Learning Strategies

Do you have strategies for each stage of the problem solving process?

Do your strategies require student input about the content, or about their learning?

Have you included directions on how to use the strategies?

Selecting a Lesson Strategy

Why Do It: Lesson Strategies for Different Instructional Purposes

As indicated at the outset of the last section, certain instructional components are necessary to learn problem solving, such as method descriptions, examples, and solution conditions. These all help a learner acquire a general problem solving method. However, these lesson components can be embodied in different types of computer teaching strategies. Also, in cases where the learner has already learned a problem solving method, certain strategies may omit some teaching components in order to focus on practice and application components.

The tutorial teaching strategy is an extremely popular method. It includes all of the lesson components of the previous section. However, there are other computer strategies that can be used, such as simulations, games, drill and practice, or problem solving tools. Simulations, games, and drill and practice require that learners solve a number of varied problems. Problem solving tools are helping strategies that can remediate and enhance a student's rule learning.

With the exception of tutorials, all of these strategies are non-instructional. They all presuppose that the student has, to some degree, already learned the rule, or is learning it from some other source (a tutorial, a teacher, etc.). Their function is to enhance or reinforce previous learning. Thus, a rule game can be used after a student has learned a rule in class, or through a deductive tutorial. All of these non-instructional strategies can be used singly, or in conjunction with inductive or deductive tutorials.

In this section, you will use a short, step-by-step guide to select the type of lesson strategy that you feel best suits your instructional needs. A variety of computer teaching strategies have been designed to serve different instructional purposes. Thus, it is important that you clarify your general lesson goals before using the guide. In particular, problem solving outcomes may not lend themselves to certain computer teaching strategies, because the problems are too lengthy or the answers are too open-ended for the computer to evaluate. This strategy selection guide will help in choosing strategy that is feasible for your lesson's problems and solutions.

You Do It: Select a Lesson Strategy

Using the guide below, answer each question and move to the step indicated by the answer:

Step 1. Does the lesson objective require that the student learn to solve a problem?

If yes, go to step 3

If no, go to step 2

Step 2. If it does not require solving a problem, go to another chapter. You do not need a problem solving lesson. You may need a lesson on rules, concepts or verbal information.

Step 3. To solve the problem, does the student apply a specific procedure?

If yes, go to step 4

If no, go to step 5

Step 4. Even though the student must solve problems, you may actually be teaching rule learning, not problem solving. Review the first part of chapter 5. If, after reviewing that section, your learning objective appears indeed to be a problem solving outcome, proceed to step 5 below.

Step 5. Have students already learned how to use a method or methods to solve problems? Are they ready to try applying the method(s)?

If they are ready to solve problems, go to step 6

If they have to learn how to solve problems, go to step 8

Step 6. How time consuming is the problem solving process? Can students apply the method to a number of different problems in a reasonable amount of time (like math problems) or can they only use it on one or two problems (like writing a poem or story)?

If you want students to apply it to a number of lesson problems, go to step 7

If you want them to apply it to only one or two, go to step 11

Step 7. You need to develop a drill and practice lesson or a game. Go to the drill/practice and game sections of this chapter. Also, see step 12.

Step 8. Will the student need to apply the problem solving methods to a wide variety of settings (school, home, work, etc.)?

For wide and varied applications training, go to step 9

For more specific situation training, go to step 10

Step 9. You need to construct a tutorial. An inductive tutorial may be best. Go to the tutorial section of this chapter. Also, see step 12 below.

Step 10. You need to construct a tutorial lesson, probably a deductive one. Go to the tutorial section of this chapter. Also, see step 12 below.

Step 11. You need to develop a problem solving simulation. Go to the simulations section of this chapter.

Step 12. Will you need to construct on-screen problem solving aids for students? These aids are tools to help students remember a problem solving method and how to apply it.

If you need such aids in your lesson, see the section on problem solving tools, after you have completed the strategy section you just selected.

If you do not think you need these aids, go to the strategy section you just selected.

This step-by-step guide is designed to help you select a teaching method for your computer lesson, but it should not be regarded as law. Once you have previewed a strategy recommended by the guide, you may want to review other strategies as well, and compare them to your chosen strategy. For example, after reviewing the section on inductive tutorials, you may also want to review the deductive tutorials section, and utilize that strategy instead. In particular, do not forget that some of these strategies can be used together, for example, tutorial followed by a simulation, or a game. Almost any tutorial can have one of the other strategies piggybacked onto it, to enhance learning and application of problem solving.

CAI Lesson Strategies

Tutorials

Why Do It: Tutorials as Primary
Teaching Strategies

Before students can solve complex problems, they usually have to learn a general method or approach to solving them. Consequently, most problem solving lessons should begin with a teaching strategy called a tutorial. Tutorials model the teaching strategies that a tutor might use to teach a student. For problem solving, the computer "tutor" must show students how they can solve problems and "watch" them as they do it, furnishing guidance.

Tutorials can be inductive or deductive. A deductive tutorial uses the computer to present problem solving guidelines and demonstrate their application. An inductive tutorial uses the computer to help the student derive (induce) guidelines for solving problems. The deductive method is easier to design, and more likely to produce learning in a shorter time. An inductive lesson may be remembered better, and transfers better to new situations the learner encounters. In some cases, the teacher may feel that the problem solving method is too complex for the student to induce, and opt for a deductive tutorial. In other cases, the teacher may want the student to discover the method/guidelines for problem solving, since the method may make more sense to the student that way.

Since inductive tutorials are more difficult to design, teachers may want to try to design such a strategy, but be prepared to "go deductive" if it is too difficult or time consuming.

How to Do It: Constructing
a Deductive Tutorial

Deductive tutorials can be constructed by following all of the lesson components and procedures outlined in the lesson components section. The tutorial should:

1. introduce the lesson and stimulate recall of prior knowledge;

2. describe the problem solving process (sub-steps/conditions);

3. demonstrate an application of the process;

4. present practice in an easy-to-hard sequence, with branching;

5. present feedback for practice.

The practice and feedback sections can also incorporate elements of simulations (see the simulations section of this chapter). That is, the practice can be done as a simulation, or a simulation can be added onto the lesson to enhance the initial lesson practice.

You Do It: Construct
a Deductive Tutorial

Go back to the lesson components section of this chapter, and follow each of the steps outlined to construct lesson components for a problem solving lesson. Make sure that all of these have a presentational mode, that is, they are being shown to the student.

For each one of the activity portions of this section, construct a series of computer screens on paper that convey that lesson component. The completed lesson should have the following components:

problem solving objective(s)

statements and descriptions of the problem solving method

characteristics of a good or bad solution to the problem

example applications with explanations

sequenced practice

feedback for right and wrong solutions to the problem

How to Do It: Constructing
an Inductive Tutorial

To construct an effective inductive tutorial, the lesson must require that students figure out the method of the problem solving approach. Students study applications of the method and generate the method's steps from the examples given. This is done by questioning students about the applications they see. The lesson poses specific questions to students about what they see, and asks them to describe it. In this sense, students tell the computer what the problem solving method is. Most inductive lessons will follow the general procedure outlined below:

Present the lesson objective.

Tell students the purpose and method of the inductive lesson. Include directions on how to answer the examples you will give them. You can include an explanation of why you want them to induce the problem solving method.

```
The Scientific Method


In this lesson you will be given
some examples of people's attempts
to solve problems. You will have to
describe the type of problem solving
activity they are doing.

By describing these activities
you will identify each step of
the scientific method.
```

Present a simple application example of one of the steps or procedures of the problem solving method. Ask students to describe or analyze the example. As an alternative, give students a general description of the step, and cue them to determine its characteristics or function:

```
Kate hypothesizes that her car
won't run because the radiator
is empty. She then opens the
radiator cap and looks in.

What is Kate doing about her
hypothesis?
```

```
The next step of the
scientific method is
testing the hypothesis.

What do you think is done
in this stage?
```

This same method can be used when there are no steps in the problem solving process. To do this, have students induce the characteristics/criteria of good and bad solutions.

Provide immediate feedback to the learners on their answers. For wrong answers, make the feedback as supportive as possible, and try to give students a second chance (with hints) before telling them the answer. For right answers, follow up the feedback with another question that requires them to induce more information about the method.

```
Your Answer: Analyze hypothesis

No, not quite. Let's try the
question again.

Think of it this way. How does
your teacher determine if you
have learned your lessons?
```

```
Very Good! This is where
one proves that the
hypothesis is right or
wrong.

How would you do that?
```

Note that the first example actually shows the student answer along with the feedback. This is a useful device when student answers are brief enough to fit onto the screen.

In many cases, a correct problem solving answer may be lengthy, or take a wide variety of forms. In these cases, it is difficult for the computer to judge student responses, and the instructor may want to design the lesson so that student answers are not judged by the computer. Instead, the lesson can tell students what their answer should have been, so students can evaluate it themselves. If students are doing the lesson in groups, or with a teacher, they can evaluate the answer together off-screen.

```
Your answer should be that
Kate is testing her hypothesis.


Did your answer involve
testing a hypothesis??

If not, press H for HELP
If so, press RETURN
```

```
Your answer: try to find out
if the hypothesis is true or
not.

Leave your answer on the
screen and go get the teacher
to look at it.  If you can't
get the teacher, write your
answer down and go on.
```

After the student has successfully induced the problem solving process, provide practice and feedback on using the method. To design practice and feedback, check the lesson components section of this chapter and review the practice and feedback lesson components.

Since problem solving methods can be difficult to induce, an inductive lesson should have some provision for showing the students the correct methodology if they cannot induce it. The computer can do it automatically, after students miss a question several times, or it can be built in as a HELP choice for students, if they run into problems.

```
    Kate was empirically
    testing her hypothesis


    This is step 3 of the method.

    Now let's try step 4.
```

```
    Did your answer mention
    the use of observation
    or experience??

    Press HELP to see answer.

    Press RETURN to try again.
```

For difficult problem solving methods, combine inductive and deductive methods. Have the student induce a simplified version of the problem solving process (or just one sub-step). Then use a deductive method to tell the student more about the method, since you feel this student could not induce this extra detail. This avoids the problem of trying to set up an entire inductive lesson on a sophisticated problem solving methodology, and yet provides the student with some inductive learning.

You Do It: Compose an Inductive Tutorial

Beginning with a screen that describes the objective, construct a draft of an inductive lesson. Construct a simple application of the method, and develop a series of screens that question the student about the method and/or its sub-steps. Be sure to include feedback frames for wrong answers to the questions, and help for students that may not induce the method. Consult the lesson components section of this chapter for practice and feedback examples:

Screen Sequence 1 (objective and directions):

Screen Sequence 2 (problems/examples of method with inductive questions):

Screen Sequence 3 (feedback to students on their inductions):

Screen Sequence 4 (practice and feedback frames):

Screen Sequence 5 (HELP and hint frames):

Games

Why Do It: Games as Motivating Practice

Problem solving games can be both challenging and interesting learning experiences for students. These games usually require that students apply problem solving methods (similar to practice exercises in tutorials), but in an atmosphere of challenge or competition. In today's computer age, many students are familiar with computer and video games, and readily use them. Consequently, computer games can be strong motivational tools for students to enhance their problem solving skills. In particular, problem solving games can be used with small groups of students on the same computer, who can reinforce each other's learning in the game.

How to Do It: Choosing the
Correct Gaming Strategy

Many problem solving games also incorporate elements of simulations in the lesson. Games involve elements of competition and chance, with rules for playing and standards for winning the game or doing well in it. Simulations mimic a real world problem solving environment that changes with decisions the student makes. Problem solving games often use real world scenarios for the student problem solving, and in that sense may be both a game and a simulation. Games and simulations are not so much separate strategies as instructional tactics that can be combined in the same problem solving lesson to improve student learning. As an analogy, think of them as spices; each can be added to the overall "recipe" of a computer lesson, and each will add its unique "flavor."

A number of challenges face the designer of problem solving games. The first is to ensure that the game in fact requires problem solving outcomes; that the students are solving problems in ways that are more than mere application of rules or concepts. The second problem is to ensure that the problem solving outcomes can be taught via a computer game.

Since many problem solving outcomes require complex and creative answers by the student, they do not easily suit a computer game format. This is because (1) the computer cannot judge the adequacy of the student's answer, (2) it is hard for students to record their work on the computer, and (3) the problem does not suit the competition/challenge atmosphere of a computer game. For example, if a student is learning to write a story, all of the preceding reasons make it unsuitable for a computer game, although a classroom storywriting competition or game might be suitable.

There are two types of problem solving scenarios that suit computer games. The first is when the problems themselves are relatively brief and require relatively specific answers. Many word problems in mathematics and the sciences fall into this category: the student must interpret the problem and "set it up" before applying any rules or principles, making it a problem solving outcome. For these problems, many of the answers are quantitative and specifiable, so that the computer can judge correctness and provide feedback. Also, the brevity of the problem means that a *series* of problems can be given students, with the computer keeping score on students' progress or achievement levels. Scorekeeping allows students to challenge or compete with others.

The other type of problem solving scenario for games devotes an entire game to the solution of one problem; students constantly employ the skills they have learned to achieve one final goal on one big problem. The game of Monopoly is a common example of this game trait, since the goal is to work creatively to achieve the most property and money by the game's end. Similarly, computer mazes and puzzles require players to work toward one final goal. For problem solving learning, a computer game of this type requires continuous application of problem solving skills, much in the same way that simulations do (see the simulations section).

If you have problem solving outcomes that suit the first type of game situation (brief problems, specific answers), complete the games section of the preceding rules chapter. For this type of problem, the game characteristics of rule learning are suitable. The only difference is that the problem solving game should include student practice on *interpreting* the problem, and practice items must require the student to set up the problem before attempting a solution.

If you have outcomes that suit the second type of situation (one continuous problem application for the whole game), follow the steps outlined below:

State the objectives and purpose of the game. Tell students how to use the game, give them basic instructions on how to proceed through the game.

```
The Scientific Detective

In this game, you will learn to
apply the scientific method to
a "case" you are on.

The object of the game is to
deduce who committed a crime,
and what the motives were.
```

```
This game will help
you learn to apply
the scientific method
to problems outside
science.
```

Additionally, you can further motivate students by describing the purpose or benefits of the game.

If possible, give the student a menu of game choices to start with. For problem solving, the student can choose to start with an easy problem, or choose the topic or context of the problem.

```
Choose Your First Case:

a. the Birthday Party Murder

b. the Missing Diamond
```

Owing to the complexity of some problem solving games, you may give the same problem to all students. In this case, make sure that the program allows the student to exit the program at any time, and/or that help is provided for students to move through the game.

Present the problem to the student. In some cases, where there are sub-steps to the problem, the game can lead off with students practicing on the first steps/stages of the problem.

```
The host of the birthday party
has been found dead. She was found
in her study.
        (GRAPHIC)
There are no signs of violence.
However, an unfinished meal
and a glass of wine were found
next to her.

What is your hypothesis? _____


_____
```

```
How do you propose to test

this hypothesis?


_____
```

Subsequent steps are used as students move through the game and solve different stages of the problem.

As students progress through the game, it should provide them with opportunities for constant interaction. Students can make choices, solve stages of the problem, or backtrack to previous decisions. As they do so, the game should provide constant feedback to the students about their choices or decisions to that point.

```
        (GRAPHIC)

 The coroner has confirmed that
 there is water in the lungs
 of the victim...

 Do you want to change your
 hypothesis???

    Press C to change...
    RETURN to go on...
```

As with all games, there must be some end point to terminate the game. This can be when the student has moved through all stages of the problem, after a certain time limit, or at the student's choice:

```
Your time is up, Detective
(name).

You have examined all the
evidence. Now you must identify
the perpetrator and describe
your reasons...
```

The game should provide feedback to students about their success. Where the problem solving answer is too open-ended for the computer to judge, teachers or students can provide the final feedback.

```
The Butler did do it. Not
the butler, but Mr. Butler!!

Press R to review your reasons
and evidence. Also, find another
"detective" and have him or her
look at your answers.
```

When constructing the game, there are some other strategies that you can build into it, depending on the nature of the lesson content. Some of these are:

"Jazz up" the game with graphics. Have the students solve problems with pictures in them, and have results graphically displayed.

Have the computer record the answers and the number of tries for each student, so you can review their performance.

Have students participate in small groups, and later do the game by themselves.

Allow students some way to exit the game before it is done, and to backtrack.

"Personalize" the game by having students enter their names at the outset of the program, and use their names in feedback messages, instructions, etc.

You Do It: Construct a Problem
Solving Game

Using the steps outlined above, construct the screens for the game, starting with the objectives and purpose of the lesson. Be sure to design a game that requires student problem solving.

Screen Sequence 1 (objectives, directions, purpose, menu):

Screen Sequence 2 (problem stages and scenarios for student to solve):

Screen Sequence 3 (student feedback and progress messages for problem stages):

Screen Sequence 4 (summary results and comments messages):

Simulations

Why Do It: Simulations for
Transfer and Retention

The majority of computer simulation software on the market today is designed to teach problem solving skills. This is because the behaviors required from simulations are essentially decision making skills for complex problems. A simulation depicts a scenario or situation that the learner would encounter in real life. Problem solving simulations require the learner to creatively apply rules, principles, or concepts to a simulated problem. As such, simulations can promote the transfer of these skills to real life situations. For example, a time economics simulation might recreate a Wall Street market scenario, where students must use economic principles to buy and sell stock.

Because simulations copy elements of real life, they also enhance the retention of problem solving skills. Students see that problem solving is applicable to real life situations, enhancing their motivation to learn. The scenarios require application of problem solving methods. This promotes skill retention. Because problem solving skills can be complex skills to learn, they require a number of application exercises for learning and retention, as well as persistence in application by the learner. Interesting simulations will motivate the learner to be persistent in applying skills to the problem at hand.

Simulations are used to enhance problem solving learning. Thus students must have already learned the applicable rules or principles before beginning the simulation. Simulations can be an excellent supplement to a tutorial, because they may provide more extensive and complex practice than a tutorial practice and feedback segment. Because they require numerous decisions by the student, simulations maintain a high level of student interaction and interest.

How to Do It: Constructing
a Simulation

As mentioned in the games section of this chapter, the attributes of games and simulations may be combined in the same problem solving lesson, and in fact often are combined. The challenge or competition elements of a game are combined with the real world features of a simulation. The key feature of simulation instruction is that a realistic scenario is provided which students must act upon, and which changes with each decision a student makes. Students must apply their skills continuously throughout the scenario in response to a number of different situations. Games and drills may provide a number of separate problems for the student, but simulations create one general problem that changes through the course of the lesson. As we said, the changing real life scenario motivates students to solve problems, and the reality of the scenario makes them feel that they are learning useful skills.

Simulations can be extremely complex to design and program, particularly where a student choice may simultaneously change a number of scenario factors. Consequently, the "How to Do It" section on simulations shows how to construct a basic simulation, one that uses simplified real life scenarios. These simplified simulations are recommended for the novice simulation designer. Commercial simulations may be more complex.

First, describe the objective and purpose of the simulation. Indicate that the student will be making decisions in the lesson:

```
Wall Street Wizard

(GRAPHIC OF WIZARD)
In this program you are
going to build a portfolio
of stocks with your own
money.

It will be your job to
buy and sell stocks on
Wall Street.
```

As with other lessons, also inform the student about the purpose and benefits of the simulation. Distinct from games, the simulation may not have a criterion for winning or achieving. Alternatively, include a goal (such as "becoming a millionaire") instead of a solution.

If possible, allow students to choose their starting point in the simulation, their role in it, or the scenario:

```
To begin, build your portfolio.
What stocks do you want to buy?
(must total $100,000)
____ shares of IBM ($100 ea)
____ shares of Kodak ($50 ea)
____ shares of Beatrice ($25)
____ $ cash reserves
____ $ of GNMA mortgage shares
```

Begin the simulation by presenting a problem scenario in which the student must choose some course of action. The scenario must require the student to creatively apply rules or concepts learned, or apply some general problem solving method:

```
The paper has just announced a
national trade deficit of $14
billion. What do you do next?
sell __ shares of _____
buy  __ shares of _____

 Press R to review prices
before buying...
```

In this case, students must apply their knowledge of marketing principles to an unencountered problem. This makes it a problem solving outcome; there is no specific rule to follow.

Have the scenario change to conform to the student's decision. The change should be based on the student's answer in such a way that the answer has caused the alteration. The new scenario should require further problem solving input from the student:

```
You purchased 50 shares of IBM,
but it dropped from $100 to
$80 with the trade deficit.

    (STOCK CHART GRAPHIC)

Press RETURN to see your
  new portfolio totals...
```

As students move through the problem simulation, they should be updated on their progress. Since problem solving answers may be quite varied and preclude specific feedback, you can tell them the *type* of progress they should have made, or the type of answers they should be giving:

```
Transactions = 6  Stock value = $60,000
Cash Reserves = $8,000

At this point you have made a number
of transactions. You should have
diversified your portfolio. If you
have not, consider the present
inflation rate (7%) before your next
purchase.
```

The simulation should continue until some logical end point is reached, one that conforms to the real life decisions the student makes. At that time, a summary judgment about student performance can be made. Where the computer may not be able to evaluate the student's problem solving performance, guidance can be given to the students to self-evaluate their performance or have someone else evaluate it:

```
In three years of transactions
your final portfolio was $145,000,
with $40,000 of it in cash.

Do you feel you turned a reasonable
profit on your transactions?

Would you have done better or
worse by investing it all in
a bank at 10% ?
```

For extensive problem solving simulations, give students the option of signing off from the computer, returning to the problem later, and picking up where they left off.

There are a number of other features that you can build into simulations to make them more effective and interesting. A few are outlined below:

The simulation can actually have "mini simulations," each of which focuses on a sub-step of a problem solving process.

After a student completes a simulation, you can hold a "debriefing" session, where the student discusses the simulation with the teacher or students. Written assignments can also be given.

For many simulations, a light touch is preferable. Try to keep the simulation humorous, while maintaining a sense of reality.

Design the simulation so that students can exit the program when they wish, or start over again.

Design HELP frames so that students can preview the problem solving method used in the simulation while they are doing it.

You Do It: Design a Problem
Solving Simulation

Using each of the steps below, design a basic simulation. Before beginning, decide on the scenario you will use, and the decision possibilities that students can make. If it seems too complex to design, look for a simpler scenario, or choose another lesson strategy such as a tutorial.

Screen Sequence 1 (explanation of objectives, purpose, and scenario):

Screen Sequence 2 (student choices to enter scenario at a certain point):

Screen Sequence 3 (first scenario, possible second scenarios based on student choices made in first scenario, third scenarios/choices, etc.):

Screen Sequence 4 (feedback on student decisions/choices for each scenario):

Screen Sequence 5 (end of simulation, summary comments):

Drill and Practice Routines

Why Do It: Drill and Practice
to Enhance Learning

Of all the different types of lesson strategies, drill and practice routines are the most application-oriented. Drills require extensive application of previously learned skills, since students apply skills to a number of problems. On the other hand, drill and practice routines assume that students already know the skills on which they will practice. As such, they effectively complement computer tutorials or classroom instruction.

A drill and practice strategy administers a problem to a student, accepts and evaluates answers to the problem, judges it as correct or incorrect, provides feedback, and administers a new problem or repeats the old one. In many cases, the strategy also records the number of times a student misses a particular question and the total number of correct and incorrect answers, thus providing information for teacher evaluation of student progress. The efficacy of drill and practice derives from the extensive practice and feedback students receive in the lesson.

While drill and practice is effective for skill development, it may not be suitable for outcomes that require students to work extensively on *only one or two* problems. It is impractical for the student to practice a large number of problems, so a drill routine is not feasible. For example, students who must learn to design a complex experiment may only do one or two "problems" for practice. Their practice problems are actually projects. They cannot drill by doing a number of projects.

Can drill and practice be used for problem solving outcomes? Yes, drills are suitable for (1) problems that have relatively specific answers and do not take too long to solve or (2) sub-steps or sub-processes of an overall problem solving method. The first type of problem is similar to rule learning problems, since there are specific answers. However, these problems require more than the simple application of rules, they require *analysis and interpretation* of the problem. Mathematics and science word problems are examples of these types of problems. They require problem solving skills, but they are actually higher order forms of rule learning, since they also require the application of rules.

The second type of problem is one where *part* of the problem solving method can be practiced in a drill. These methods have distinct sub-steps that each must be applied creatively to solve the overall problem. For example, the scientific method is a problem solving method that does not lend itself wholesale to drill and practice, but a sub-step such as "defining the problem" could be drilled separately. Similarly, writing a story is a non-drill problem solving outcome, but writing a topic sentence for the story (a sub-process) can be drilled. After students have drilled on the sub-steps, they can do one or two "big" problems that use all the sub-steps.

Thus, the first step in designing a problem solving drill is to make sure that your outcome is amenable to a drill and practice routine. If not, consider a tutorial or simulation strategy that is suitable for complex or open-ended problems. If a drill is suitable, follow the general guidelines described below.

How to Do It: Constructing a
Problem Solving Drill

Basic drill and practice routines are relatively easy to design, but there are a number of subtle techniques that should be incorporated into effective drills to make them truly effective. A good drill and practice routine does more than simply present a problem and confirm that an answer is right or wrong. Effective problem solving drills should contain the following features:

A description of the purpose and objectives of the drill, followed by directions.

A practice sequence that requires creative problem solving through use of the general problem solving method or one of its sub-steps.

Problems that vary in difficulty and content. The problems can increase in difficulty, or students can choose a difficulty level.

Feedback to students that either confirms the correctness of their answers, cues them to the type of correct answers, or allows them to evaluate their own answers.

Review of practice items, where a missed problem is repeated immediately or later on in the drill.

Student recordkeeping, where the computer records and reports student performance to the teacher and/or student.

The essential purpose of the drill is to furnish the student with informed practice in problem solving. Drills are similar to the basic practice and feedback routines of tutorials, but usually have more practice.

Begin the drill by giving the student an overview of the upcoming lesson, including the lesson objective/purpose, and directions on how to use the computer drill.

```
Drill 1: The Writer's Workshop

This drill will help you learn
to write complex and compound
sentences.

     (GRAPHIC)

To do this you will adapt the
grammar and usage principles
you learned in the last lesson.
```

```
You will be given a
sentence topic, and
instructions to write
a certain type of
sentence on the topic.

You will then compose
a sentence of that type.
```

The overview can also explain the purpose or benefits of the drill, better motivating students to learn it.

Introduce the first practice problem. The problem can require the use of the entire method, or it can be practice on a sub-step of the method. Your choice depends on the type of problem solving outcome you teach. In either case, the first problem should be relatively easy, with harder ones to follow.

Easy problem using entire method   *Easy problem using sub-step*

```
Problem 1: Tom's Dog

Write a complex sentence with
one dependent clause.

The main clause subject is Tom.
The object is his dog Annabelle.

The verb is "feeds."

The dependent clause is about
her persnickety eating habits.
```

```
Step 2 Practice: Defining

Felice leaves the house to
go to work. She gets in her
car, and it won't start.

Write a problem definition

_____:
```

You can also create a series of easy, harder, and difficult problems, and allow the students to select the difficulty level they want to start with. This works well when students vary widely in problem solving ability.

Present a series of problems to the student. Problems should vary in difficulty (even within difficulty levels), and should range across all contexts where the rule would be applied. Generally, you should use an easy-to-hard problem sequence. As indicated in the preceding example, all problems should be numbered so the student can track the number of problems completed.

Present feedback messages to the student for each attempted solution. Feedback should be given to students for both right and wrong answers, similar to the feedback messages in the lesson components section. If the problem solution is too variable for the computer to judge, provide an example of the correct solution. If the solution is predictable enough for the computer to judge, cue students who miss the answer, and give them another try:

Examples feedback   *Cued feedback*

```
Your answer should look
something like this:

Tom feeds his dog Annabelle,
who is a picky eater.

Does your main clause have
Tom feeding Annabelle? If not,
Press R to rewrite.
```

```
Not Quite.

The definition should deal
with her work or job.

 Try again   (RETURN)
```

Branch students to the same or a different problem after feedback. Use several branching strategies depending upon students' answers and their number of tries. When students miss an item, either (a) give them the answer and give them a new problem, (b) tell them how they were incorrect and let them try it again immediately, or (c) tell them how they were incorrect and have them try it again later, after three to six other drill problems:

```
Your definition is
a little too narrow.


Later, we'll try this
problem again.
```

```
            Your answer: How to start the
            car.

            You should have defined this
            problem in a broader sense,
            dealing with her job.

            RETURN to do problem again.
```

As a rule, have students try the problem again before giving them the answer. Arrange special branches for students who are doing well in the program. If they have solved a number of problems on the first try (particularly if they are difficult ones) the computer can count these answers/tries and send the student out of the program or into more difficult problems.

As a close to the drill, give students feedback about their overall performance. This can include number or percentage of problems correct, and the number of tries:

```
    Drill 2: Problem Definition

        Final Score:

    You solved 2 easy probs.
    on the first try, 2 on second.

    You solved 1 of 2 difficult
    probs. on the first try, 1
    on second.

        Would you like to try again?
```

Where students have not completed most of the problems, you can have them try the drill again. As indicated, the computer can store students' performance records for you to look at later.

There are several other features that you can build into the drill to enhance its learning effectiveness:

The computer can randomize the presentation of problems, so that no student gets the same sequence. This can even be done within difficulty levels.

Vary the contexts of application in the problems. Can the method be applied to work, school, home problems?

Problem solving tools can be built into the drill (see problem solving tools section).

You Do It: Construct a Problem Solving Drill

Beginning with the introductory drill screens, outline a drill and practice routine on paper. Begin with the introductory frames and move to the practice and feedback frames. Remember that drills require a number of varied problems, and a variety of feedback messages and branches. The same screen can contain both feedback and information about where the student will be branched:

Screen Sequence 1 (objectives, purpose, menu of choices):

Screen Sequence 2 (entire problems or sub-step problems, in easy-to-hard sequence):

Screen Sequence 3 (feedback and branching messages to students for correct and incorrect answers):

Screen Sequence 4 (remedial or help frames for errors):

Screen Sequence 5 (scores and summary feedback):

Problem Solving Tools for Problem Solving Learning

Why Do It: Problem Solving Tools
Aid Acquisition and Application

Problem solving tools should not be confused with problem solving outcomes. Problem solving outcomes are specific types of learning, different from concepts and rules. Problem solving tools are instructional aids that are used for all types of learning outcomes: rules, concepts, problem solving, even verbal information. These tools are instructional adjuncts to tutorials, games, simulations, and drills. They help students learn and practice a given learning outcome. For problem solving outcomes, students use a problem solving tool to remind them of the problem solving process, or to cue them about acceptable problem solving solutions.

Problem solving tools are aids embedded in the computer program itself. They help the student solve the problem of mastering the learning outcome. For problem solving outcomes, problem solving tools take a variety of forms. They can be used to review a process such as the scientific method. They can also furnish guidelines for problem solutions, such as a checklist of characteristics of a good haiku. The tool can also be a list of principles or heuristics for checking the sub-steps of the solution process, to ensure that it is properly conducted.

Problem solving tools are useful guides for problem solving, especially for the novice problem solver. They provide the kind of on-screen help that a teacher might give to a student who was stuck on a problem. However, with a problem solving tool the student can get help anytime without leaving the computer program. As with many on-screen aids, the tool can model the way an expert would solve the problem, or the information an expert would use.

There are a wide variety of simple and sophisticated problem solving tools for computer lessons. For our purposes, we review one of the most basic and important tools for problem solving learning, the use of an on-screen aid.

How to Do It: Constructing an On-Screen
Aid for Problem Solving

The aid should help students utilize a problem solving method or guidelines. To do this, the aid can focus on reviewing the characteristics of a good solution. This can help students judge if they have applied the process correctly, without telling them the answer:

Scientific method solution check

```
Does your solution:

    Solve the problem of getting
    to work, not fixing the car?

    Allow for verifiability by
    testing or observation?
```

This example contains a checklist. Checklists are popular forms of on-screen aids. With a checklist, you ask students about their solution, encouraging them to question themselves about solution characteristics. This aid is similar to the self-check units in this chapter.

As an alternative to reviewing the solution characteristics, you can use an example of a problem solution, as described in the lesson components section of this chapter. The example aid can be used in problem solving practice. Students can generate correct solutions that are similar, but not identical to the example.

For problem solving methods with sub-steps, another alternative is to make an aid available that reviews the method and its sub-steps. This would be similar to the problem solving presentation strategies outlined in the first part of the lesson components section.

Decide when the aid will be available to the student. You can make it available throughout the program, or only for initial problem applications, such as the first two or three problems in a drill, tutorial, simulation, or game:

```
(Triangle
Graphic)
            Problem # 2

            Prove that drawing a line
            perpendicular to the base side
            of an isosceles triangle creates
            two congruent triangles.

                    Press H for HELP
                    before you answer.
```

Students can review the aid before they try to solve the problem, and then come back to the problem. If you have several aids designed for students (example review, sub-step review), you can have different keystroke choices for each one. For example, "Press H to review method," "Press E to see an example," etc.

You Do It: Construct a Problem
Solving Tool

Review your lesson's practice problems. Decide on an aid or aids that will help students when they are solving each problem. If possible, organize the aid into an on-screen tool that will be part of the computer lesson. If it will not fit into the computer, make it available as a print accompaniment to the lesson.

Screen Sequence 1 (solution characteristics or example solutions):

Screen Sequence 2 (other aids):

Special Software Tools
for Problem Solving Learning

A variety of commercial software tools, often referred to as *utility software*, can be used as problem solving tools. These are particularly useful when the learner must learn a *set* of related rules or principles in one lesson, such as a set of addition, grammar, or musical notation rules. This utility software can then be used to learn the sub-skills that must be learned to master problem solving, such as rules or concepts. For examples of these utility software tools, consult the database management tools sections of chapters 3, 4, and 5.

Expert systems are artificial intelligence programs that consist of a set of "if-then" decisions that simulate the decision making skills of an expert. An expert system can contain the appropriate steps that an expert would use to solve a problem. These systems are mainly useful for mimicking problem solving behavior.

The instructional strength of expert systems lies in students' design of the expert system. Using special computer authoring systems to create the expert system, students outline and describe the procedures an expert problem solver would undertake to solve the problem. The process of producing the aid is as important as the product, since the student comes to better understand and apply the rules of the expert system.

For further information about expert systems, read some of the sources listed in the bibliography in the back of this book.

Evaluating Problem Solving Tutorials

Most of the CAI software created and used by teachers is tutorial, rather than simulations, games, etc. Therefore, we have included a brief section on how to evaluate a problem solving tutorial. When designing a problem solving tutorial, review it using the evaluation checklist in this section. The checklist can also be used as an evaluation tool for commercial tutorial software.

When evaluating commercial software, the first question to ask is "Does the lesson teach problem solving outcomes?" This cannot be judged by reading the program title or its instructions, even if it says that it is a problem solving lesson. It can only be done by trying out the program itself, to see if it actually teaches the problem solving based on application of specified rules or procedures. Sometimes, a purported problem solving lesson will actually teach rule using, or concept learning.

Evaluation Checklist
(Answer each question by checking one of three categories:)

	None	Adequate	Very Good
1. Requires creation of solution?			
2. Readiness activities provided?			
3. Problem solving process guidelines outlined?			
4. Examples of application provided?			
5. Examples explained?			
6. Practice provided?			
7. Logical means for evaluating practice?			
8. Cues or help for problem solution?			
9. Branching?			

If you have created your own program, it is critical that you find several sample students and try out the program on them. Sit down next to a student and watch him or her try out the program. Take notes, make corrections, and do it again with another student. This can be done when the program is coded into the computer, or when it is still on paper. Either way, this will help reveal any problems with the lesson before using it for instruction.

Summary

Problem solving involves the creative use of rules and concepts to solve complex problems. In some cases there are general methods to use; in others there are only guidelines. All effective problem solving lessons have a certain set of lesson components, whether they are taught on the computer or not. In particular, problem solving lessons must offer guidance to the student problem solver, and feedback suited to the complexity and generality of the solutions generated. Computer tutorials, deductive and inductive, are the most effective methods for learning problem solving on the computer, while drills and games are less feasible for complex problems. To develop and enhance problem solving performance, simulations, games, and drills can be used as an adjunct to tutorials.

Part 3

Enhancing the Basic CAI Lesson

Chapter 7
Designing User Interactions in Courseware

What makes computer-based instruction distinctive from traditional instruction is the interactivity of the instruction. Rather than passively receiving instructional presentations, learners can interact with the presentation. The Greeks believed that the best instruction is dialogue. In well-designed computer-based instruction (CBI), the learner engages in a dialogue with the computer program. The more dynamic the interaction is, the more active the learner will be. We have stated repeatedly that active processing of information improves learning. So the key to designing good CBI is to make sure that courseware engages the learner in a meaningful and dynamic interaction.

This chapter is designed to help you to "embellish" your basic program design that you have produced in previous chapters. Use the hints in this chapter to revise the design and add details.

User Interface Principles

Make the user interface interactive. Allow the learner to make choices. Make choices meaningful so the learner responds in a meaningful way. If the only learner response is "Press Space Bar to Continue," your dialogue is really a monologue. Allow students to make choices about what they see next, how many examples they want, what types of practice items they want, and so on.

Anticipate any possible user errors and design a message that explains the error to the user. Sometimes, a student will know the correct answer but make an error in entering it. Anticipate errors in key pressing, misinterpretation of directions, or misconception of the task. Create an error handler routine which recognizes as many errors as you can anticipate and presents a message to the learner about how to recover from the error. This subroutine should be run automatically whenever the learner is asked to respond for any reason, so that it can be used over and over in the same lesson. To construct an error handling routine, simply repeating the screen which prompted the learner error is not enough. This is because users will not know what to do or why they made a mistake. They end up in a loop making the same mistake over again and becoming increasingly frustrated.

Show the error screen and then show a prompt screen. The prompt screen tells the viewer the type of response that is required or the options that the user has so the users will now know how to properly respond.

```
        PROBLEM!

You have made a response that cannot be
recognized. When the question is displayed
again,

     Type in your response.
     Check your spelling.
     If correct, press Return.
     If incorrect, press <- key and retype.
```

```
You have made a response that

cannot be recognized.
-------------------------------
You must press one of the
following keys:

     H for Help
     A for Answer
     F for Feedback
```

In some prompt screens, you can even show the learner the *type* of answer that you expect (e.g., "Please answer in the form Ax + b = c"). This tells users how to enter their answers.

Design the interfaces in accordance with the learner's level of ability or knowledge. When you are designing a program for beginners, give short, precise, and explicit directions, such as "First, do this.... Next, do this...." If your learners are more experienced with the topic, then you may expect more prior knowledge about system operations and will not have to prompt them as much.

Test the system with target learners until it works dependably. Before using the courseware to teach, try it out with learners from the target audience (learners of the same age, ability, motivation, etc., for whom you are developing the courseware). Begin by observing a learner using the software. Have the learner work through the lesson while thinking aloud, expressing reactions to the problem. Note where the learner hesitates, becomes confused, or is totally lost. Query the learner about why he or she is having problems. Revise the courseware and try it out with several other learners. Later, do not intercede. Make sure that the learner can work through the lesson and learn independently. After it works dependably, then and only then use it to instruct. *Don't ever assume that learners will be able to figure it out.* It is amazing how learners, even educated, adult learners, can misinterpret poorly communicated intentions.

Interactivity in the Interactions

We said earlier that the key to good CBI is interactivity. Interactivity implies meaningful transactions between the learner and the lesson. The type of activity that you ask the learner to engage in, more than anything else, will determine what the learner learns.

Be sure that the learner's actions are consistent with the task stated in the objective or with a task level of a sub-objective. You have learned to classify the level of learning required by each of the tasks identified by the instructional analysis. When teaching that sub-objective, make sure the practice items match the level of information-tion processing stated in the objective. If the objective or sub-objective is a verbal information task, make sure that the interactions call for verbal information. If the objective or sub-objective calls for concept, make sure that the activities call for classification of new instances. And so on....

Provide the learner with a reasonable number of attempts to complete the task. Key pressing and spelling errors are common. If you can anticipate those and provide feedback accordingly, great. Learners should have at least two attempts at an answer. However, after three attempts, the learner deserves prompting or help. After four attempts, forget it.

If spelling or punctuation is not important, design the computer lesson to accept answers with these errors (e.g., to accept "lincon" for "Lincoln").

```
The second line of your haiku is still
----------------------------------------
   incorrect.
   ----------

Slowly recite the second line aloud.

How many syllables does it have?
```

```
Your answer, reinforcement, was incorrect.
-------------------------------------------

First, check the spelling.

If spelled correctly, your answer
is incorrect.

When the question is displayed again,
   type the correct response followed
   by RETURN.
```

Provide enough interaction or practice to set the learning. How many practice items or how much interaction is provided for the learner depends upon the role of the question in instruction. If an interaction is inserted merely to maintain the learner's attention, one response of each type will probably do. If, however, the interaction is a practice item (learning guidance) for a difficult task, there should be three or more problems. The jury is still out on exactly how many practice items are necessary. A good rule of thumb for new learning is three or four items. More may be needed for very complex material or for drill and practice sequences.

Require that the learner make the appropriate response. Even if you have to present the answer to the learner after four or more attempts, present the activity again and require the learner to make the correct response. It is important that the learner practices making the correct response.

```
The second step in the

Salami Principle is to

slice the task into small

bites.
```

```
What is the second

step in the Salami

Principle?

_____
```

Provide enough meaningful options for learner to make the lesson a true learning experience. Learning with a tutor or in a classroom usually entails a greater variety of interactions between the teacher and learners than display-question-feedback CAI. Learners may engage in a variety of information seeking behavior. So, courseware too should provide more information seeking options to the learner. At any time during the lesson, learners should be provided some or all of the following options:

- help key to get procedural information

- answer key for answering a question

- glossary key for seeing a definition of any term

- objective key for reviewing the course objective being worked on.

- content map key for accessing an overview map of the content in the course or lesson and how it fits together (see the hierarchical menu principles on pages 204-6).

- options key for seeing a list of learner commands or options available to the learner

- overview or introduction key for reviewing the introduction to the unit

- menu key for exiting the lesson and returning to menu

- exit key for exiting the course and leaving

- summary key for seeing the summary or conclusions of the lesson

- review key for reviewing parts of the lesson

- comment key for recording a learner comment about the lesson, i.e., taking notes

- examples key for seeing examples of an idea

- previous frame or next frame for moving forward or backward in a lesson

- test key for letting the program know when the learner is ready to take a test

- next lesson key for accessing the next lesson in a sequence

These are most often implemented by having the learner use control keys, that is, hold down the CONTROL or ESCAPE key while pressing a mnemonically coded key. For instance, Control-G for glossary, Control-E for exit, and so on. Options or functions may also be presented in a menu of options or in an option line on the screen. Using a sub-routine to analyze the learner's key press and respond accordingly saves time and programming effort.

```
The second step in the Salami
Principle is to slice the task
into small bites.
-------------------------------
<CTL>E for an Example
<CTL>Q for a Question
<CTL>O for Objective
<CTL>M for Menu
<CTL>N for Next frame
```

Adaptation in Learner Interactions

Another important characteristic of a good tutor or teacher is the ability to adapt instruction to individual learners. Courseware can do the same. Screens and lessons can be designed to adapt instruction in a variety of ways. Instructional events may be under learner control (where the learner makes the decisions) or they may be under program control (where the computer makes the decisions). Under program control, the computer may adapt the quantity or quality of instruction based upon the learners' needs. Slower learners need more help. More adept learners need less help. Or the program may arbitrarily assign learners to a "fat" version of the course, that is, a version that contains the maximum amount of instructional support and information. Everyone should receive all of the instruction possible, right? Wrong! Additional instruction will not help some learners and may even impede others. In order to save time, the program may also assign the learner to a "lean" version, instruction that provides only the minimum. Much research shows that lean versions of instruction may be just as effective as fatter versions. What kinds of instructional events may be controlled by the learner or the program? Figure 7.1 lists a number of instructional variables crossed with the control options described above.

	Levels of Control			
Types of Adaptation	**Learner Control**	**Program Control**		
		Adaptive	**Fat**	**Lean**
Content Selected				
Instructional Support:				
Number of examples				
Number of practice items				
Difficulty level of practice items				
Sequence of Instruction:				
Inductive-Deductive				
General-Specific				
Easy-Hard				
Context of Instruction:				
Personalized				
Preferentially Selected				
Type of Feedback:				
Level of Feedback				
Positive-Negative				
Corrective-Remedial				
Analytical				
Knowledge of Results				
Advisement				
Incentives				

Figure 7.1. Forms of adaptive instructional treatments in CBI.

As should be obvious from this table, many options for adapting instruction exist. In the principles presented below, we describe only a few of the more prominent methods for adapting instruction to learners.

Provide learners maximum control of their learning options. Learners may be allowed to control the pace, sequence, and nature of instruction using some or all of the options listed in the fifth principle in the last section. This is a philosophically and pedagogically pleasing idea. Let the learner control his or her fate. Knowledge is individually constructed, so the individual learner knows best what he or she needs. The only problem occurs when learners are not mature or motivated enough to make wise choices. Research has shown that those who benefit from more instruction (the less capable learners) are the ones who usually choose the minimum of instruction or the wrong type of instruction and those who need it the least (high achievers) opt for more instruction. Be careful. Learner control may reduce learning. Provide only those choices that the learners are capable of making.

Advise learners about the choices they should make. Learner control can be made more effective by advising learners on the kinds of choices they should make, while still providing the learner the option of making it. If we know that less able learners need more instruction, we can advise them, based upon pretest scores, that they should try additional practice items, etc.

```
Would you like to see another

example?

      Yes          No
```

```
We recommend that you

try five practice items.

Do you agree?

      Yes    No
```

Be careful here, too. Even with advice, learners do not make the best decisions. The advice may be used to present the requisite amount of instructional support without providing the learner with the option of choosing whether to follow it.

Provide more instructional support under program control for less able learners and less instruction for more capable learners. It is not difficult to vary the amount of instructional support, i.e., the number of examples or the number of practice items, to match the needs of the learner. Learners with more prior knowledge (higher pretest scores) need less learning guidance as well as fewer examples and practice items than learners with less ability or prior knowledge. There are several mathematical equations for determining the amount of instruction that is needed. The simplest is to provide the number of examples and/or practice items that is the reverse of the learner's pretest score. For instance, if the lesson includes a 7-item pretest, learners scoring 7 would need only one example or practice item. Learners scoring 6 would get two items each, and so on down to learners scoring 0 or 1 on the pretest. They would get all 7 examples and practice items. Students with high pretest scores can also start out with more complex examples as well as fewer ones.

Vary the context of instructional support to meet the needs or interests of the learners. Research has shown that learners comprehend instruction better when the instruction refers to information with which they are familiar. Another way of adapting the lesson to the learner is to vary the context or subject of the information. For instance, when teaching a lesson on arithmetic averages, present examples or practice items that deal with batting averages, ages of classmates, Girl Scout cookie sales, or a variety of contexts, allowing the learner to

```
Problem 3

If Duke Snider, No. 67, was at

bat 623 times last season, and he

hit safely 207 times, what was his

batting average?

> . __ __ __
```

```
Problem 3

Girl Scout Troop No. 67 sold 623

boxes of cookies this year. Debbie

sold 207 of those boxes. What portion

of the total did Debbie sell?

> . __ __ __
```

choose the subjects of examples or practice items. The *information* is the same; only the *context* changes. Learning increases. Also, motivation and interest increase and possibly the transfer of learning as well.

Menu Design

After entering most restaurants, you are usually presented with a menu which communicates the food options. The simplest menus provide only a single sequence of choices. It is chicken Dijon, steak Diane, or vegetarian medley. More sophisticated menus require a series of decisions, such as a selection of appetizers, soups, entrées, desserts, wines, etc. The more complicated the menu, the more difficult are the decisions, especially if the food is well prepared. The menu is a useful metaphor for describing and communicating the variety of learner options available to learners in computer-based instruction or in using most computer software. Menus help learners to make choices, which increases their interest and individualizes instruction.

The menu is a means for presenting a sequence of options requiring learner decisions. Computer software menus usually require only one decision at a time, however. Making one decision may lead to another set of options or to some action by the computer. Menus are the most common logical interface between the user and the computer. Because of this, it is imperative that they be well designed. Designing menus is harder than it looks. In menu design, Murphy's Law prevails: If it is possible to misinterpret a direction or intention, someone will. In designing menus, the designer must convert the logic of the computer into simplified, linear, human logic. Quite a feat of translation. Menus must make a program easier to use, not harder. Navigating through menus is one of the most significant "human factors" problems facing the CBI designer. The following principles may help with the task.

Design menus with a clear model of the learner in mind. Menu complexity needs to vary with the sophistication of the user. For neophytes, the menu needs to be clear and simple to use, with direct command options.

```
                Your Options
------------------------------------------

1   Do you want to see more examples
    of solidification?

2   Do you want to try identifying
    instances of solidification?

3   Do you want to review the
    definition of solidification?

4   Do you want to quit?

------------------------------------------

Press the number of your choice.
```

```
                        TORTS Menu
        ------------------------------------------
        History of Torts
        Filing a Tort in court
        Parties in a Tort action
        Laws affecting the resolution
        When to file a Tort
        ------------------------------------------
        Type the underlined letter to begin
        the lesson of your choice.
```

Be consistent, active, and clear in the way you present options to the learner. Use parallel structure in presenting options. Preferably, begin each option with an action verb that states what the program will do or allow the user to do if he or she selects that option (e.g., answer questions, review the program, look up a term). Select verbs that are clear and descriptive. The structure of the phrase describing each option should be the same. Do not abbreviate any of the options. Remember, when in doubt, be explicit. See the example in the sixth principle in this section.

Provide the user with feedback about the selection by confirming their choice or writing the option title on the next screen. A good rule of thumb suggests that every response by the learner deserves some feedback. So when a learner makes a selection, confirm that selection. This is especially important if the selection results in a delay of several seconds while the program loads from the disk. Rather than facing a blank screen, the learner knows that the computer is responding properly to the selection. If the selection causes a jump within a program, the title of the next screen should be worded similarly to the selection.

```
                You selected

        Try a practice item


            One moment please.
            Getting that practice item.
```

```
                Practice Item
            ----------------------

        Is the following description an example
        of positive reinforcement?

                Type Y or N

        ------------------------------------------
        |                                        |
        |   Suzanne has been gradually           |
        |   withdrawing the food treats that     |
        |   she gives her dog when he sits up.   |
        |                                        |
        ------------------------------------------
```

Highlight the keywords (actions) resulting from each option. Use italics, inverse, underlining, or a different color text to signal the primary action that will result from the selection of that option.

```
        CHOOSE an option

        RELATE it to other topics
```

Use numbers, not bullets or letters, for presenting options in a menu list. If the options are not highlighted, then use numbers. Do not insert periods, brackets, or parentheses after the numbers. The user can become confused about the response that is required. He or she will not know whether to respond with a "2" or a "2.".

```
      Select an option by typing

      the number of the action

      that you want.

      -----------------------------------

  1   Review the definition of the Salami
      Principle

  2   See a demonstration of the Salami
      Principle

  3   Try applying the Salami Principle
      to a practice task
```

Design menus to fit the processing needs of the user, that is, group similar options together and present the most frequently used options first. The organization of options within any menu list should be grouped categorically. Similar functions or options should be grouped together. Spatially separate the groups by extra space between the groups. The options that are most likely to be selected should be listed first or designated as the default option. The default option is the menu option that is highlighted when the menu appears or the one that is automatically selected if the learner simply presses return. The default option is usually the first option presented. Options may also be grouped by the order in which they should be used (if such a sequence is predictable). Avoid alphabetical ordering; it is usually an arbitrary arrangement.

```
                    Student Response Options

      Select the option that you want to do.

      Then press the number next to that option.
      ------------------------------------------------

      1   See new examples of reinforcement
      2   See previous examples of reinforcement

      3   Review definition of reinforcement
      4   Review course objective
      5   Review last screen

      6   Try a practice item
```

No menu (main menu or sub-menus) in hierarchical menu structures should contain more than eight options. When the menu contains eight or more options that can be grouped in two or more clusters, develop a hierarchical menu. A hierarchical menu clusters options together into sub-menus. The user requests an option by first requesting the sub-menu which contains the option and then selecting the specific option. Hierarchical menus are needed for complex programs which contain many options. Their purpose is to reduce the number of options that a user has to consider at one time. The most important task for the menu designer is to group options together meaningfully into coherent sub-menus.

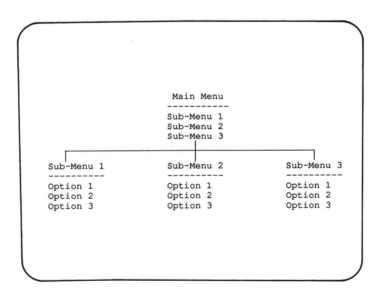

Hierarchical menu structures should be no more than three levels deep. The main menu may call two or more sub-menus, which in turn may call two or more sub-menus. If all sub-menus contain 8 options, this results in as many as 64 options, a very complex program indeed. Such a program would likely be confusing to the user before even starting the lesson.

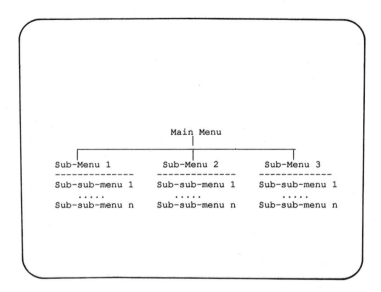

Hierarchical menus may call action options or content options. Hierarchical menus have a variety of uses. They make navigating through a program simpler. They also provide an overview of the lesson to help prepare the learner for new knowledge (see part 1 of this book).

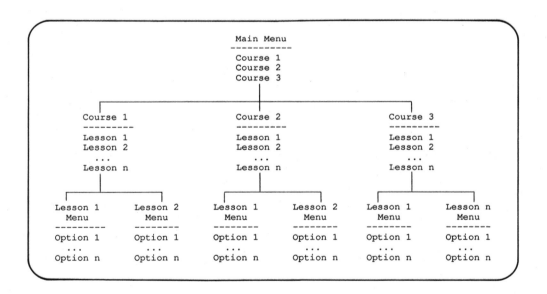

When using a hierarchical menu, make a menu map (a graphic organizer of the menu structure). The map shows the array of options available to the learner and how they all fit together and how they are all accessed. This map should be available to the user at all times to help in determining the current location and navigating through the menu structure.

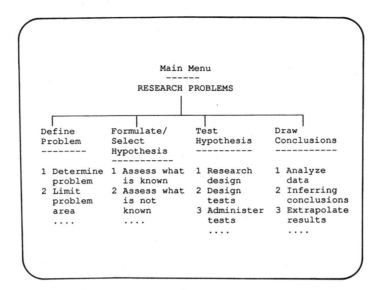

```
                        Main Menu
                        ------
                   RESEARCH PROBLEMS


  Define         Formulate/      Test          Draw
  Problem        Select          Hypothesis    Conclusions
  --------       Hypothesis      ----------    -----------
                 ----------
  1 Determine    1 Assess what   1 Research    1 Analyze
    problem        is known        design        data
  2 Limit        2 Assess what   2 Design      2 Inferring
    problem        is not          tests         conclusions
    area           known         3 Administer  3 Extrapolate
  ....           ....              tests         results
                                 ....          ....
```

Options that should be available in every menu are "Return to the next higher level menu" or if at the main menu, "Exit from the program." In navigating through an elaborate menu structure, users need to be able to move vertically in order to move laterally. Therefore, users need to be able to get to a higher level menu in order to select the option which will allow them to select another option on another menu. The most common method is to move up to a higher level menu, select another sub-menu, and then select the option that is desired. At the highest level, the main menu, the user should be able to escape from the program, that is, to exit.

```
              TEST HYPOTHESIS MENU

               Program Segments
               ----------------------

       1   Design research project

       2   Design tests

       3   Administer tests

       4   Escape to Main Menu
```

For advanced users, provide direct access to alternative options—permit the user to move, with familiarity, from menus to mnemonics. Hierarchical menu structures make navigating through a complex piece of software much easier for new users. However, after the user has gained familiarity with a program, moving vertically and laterally through the menu structure in order to select another option of the program becomes a nuisance. For instance, in the example above, if the learner were studying option 2, Limit Problem Area, under Define Problem and wanted to study the Define Tests section under Test Hypotheses, he or she would have to go back up through the Define Problem menu to the main menu, select the Test Hypothesis menu, and then select section 2 from that menu. The advanced user should be able to go immediately from one section of the program to another without having to navigate through the menu structure. Many complex programs provide the user the opportunity to move laterally with a single command, rather than escaping upward, across the menu structure, and then down to the option he or she wants. This can be done by assigning control keys (e.g., Control-K) or module numbers (e.g., 2.2) to various options, so that by pressing Control-K or 2.2, for instance, that option is immediately shown to the learner.

Summary

There are two types of learner interactions in CAI: interaction with the instructional components and interaction with the computer program. In this chapter, we have presented and illustrated a number of principles for designing both types of interactions. The more of these principles that you incorporate into your computer lesson, the more effective they will be. By now, you should have designed your instructional events and strategies and sequenced those in a drill, tutorial, simulation, or problem solving program. Review your program and then review the principles in this chapter to see if you cannot improve the learner interactions in your instructional program.

Chapter 8
Designing Screen Presentations

Reading information from a computer screen is substantially different from reading information on a printed page. There are problems related to the resolution of the screen (acuteness or quality of the images), the luminance level of the screen, the contrast of images, and the amount of information that can be included on a screen. Human factors researchers and information scientists have studied methods for arranging and displaying information on a computer screen. Researchers have studied the physiological effects of reading from a computer terminal for long periods of time (the ergonomic factors). Although many principles for designing screens have resulted from this research, screen design remains somewhat of an art.

Research has shown that computer screens can be designed to provide a sense of order or structure, a sense of simplicity, and a sense of spaciousness. Structured, simple, spacious screens are generally preferred by users of CBI.

Designing Structured Screens

If information is to be comprehended and memorized, it must be organized by the learner. If it is not organized as it is encoded into memory, the information will not be easy to retrieve from memory at some later time. The screen designer can help the user structure the information as it is committed to memory as well as accessing information from the screen by organizing or structuring the information on the screen. The following principles illustrate techniques for how to structure information on the screen. The following examples use the notation method to simulate computer screens. That is, they use X's and O's to illustrate layout characteristics independent of the content being presented.

Use one or more lines on each screen to provide orientation information. Provide screen numbers, subject headings, or descriptors to let learners know where in the overall subject content they are. Show students what commands are available, or information about how well the learner is doing. These examples show two versions of highly structured screens with orientation information at the top of the screen.

```
┌─────────────────────────────────────────────────────────────────┐
│  ┌──────────────────────────────────────────────────────────┐   │
│  │ oooo oooo      oo ooooooooo ooo oooo o oooo ooooo oooo  ii│   │
│  │ xx       x xx       x xx       x xx      xxx xxxxx    xxxxxx xxx xxxxxx│   │
│  └──────────────────────────────────────────────────────────┘   │
│   ooooooooooo   xx xxx xxxxxx x xx xx xxx xxxxxxxx x xxxxx xx xxx xxxx  │
│                 xxxxxxxx xx xxx xxxx xxxx xx xxxxx xxxx xxxxxxxx xxxx    │
│                 xxxxx xxxxxxxxx xxxxxxx xxxx xxxxx xxxx xxx xxxx xxxx xx x│
│                 xxxx xxxxx xxxxx xxxxxxxx xxxx xxx xxx xx xxxxxxx xxxxx  │
│                 xxxx xxx xxxx xxxxx xxxxxx xxxx                         │
│                                                                        │
│   ooooooooo      xxx xx xxx xxx xxxxxxxxx xxxx xxxxxxx xxx xx xxxxx xxxx x│
│   oooo ooo       xxxxxx xxxxxx xx xxxxxx xxxxxxxxx xxx xx xxx xxxx xxxx xxxx│
│   oo ooooo       xxxxxx xxx xxxxxxx xx xx xxxxx xx xxxxx xxx xxxx xxxxxx xx│
│                  xxxxx xx xxx xxxxx xxx xxxxxx xx xxx xxxx xxxx xxxx xxxxx│
│                  xx xxxxx xxx xxxxx xxx xxxxx xxxxxxx xxx xxxxxxxx xxxxx xxx│
│                  xx xxx xxxx                                            │
│                                                                        │
│   oooo oooo      xxxxx xxxx xx xxxx x xxxxxx xxxxxx xxxxxx xxx xxxx xxxxx│
│   ooooooooo      xxxxxx xxxxxx xx xxxx xxxxx xxxx xx xxx xxxxxxxx        │
│   oo ooooo       xxxxxxx xx xxxx xxxxxxxx xxxxx xxxxxxxxx xxxxxxxxx xxxxxxx│
│                  xxxxxxxx xxx xxx xxx xxxxx xx xxxxxxx xx xxxx x xxxxxx   │
│                  xxxx xxx xxxxxxx xxxx xxxxxx xx xxxxx xxxxxxxxxxxxxx    │
│                  xxx xx x xxxxxxx xxx xxx xxxx xxx xxx xx xxx xxxxx      │
│                  xxxxxxxxxxxxxx                                         │
└─────────────────────────────────────────────────────────────────┘




        ┌───────────────────────────────────────────────────┐
        │   ┌───────────────────────────────────────────┐   │
        │   │ oo ooooooooo ooooooo ooo ooooooooooo   ii │   │
        │   │ xx     x xx  x  xx         xxx xxxxxx      │   │
        │   └───────────────────────────────────────────┘   │
        │   ooooo ooooooooo ooo oooo                         │
        │   xxxxxx xx x xxxx xxxx xx xxx x xxxx xx x         │
        │   xxxx xxxxx xx xxx xxxxxxxxx xxxxxxx              │
        │   xxxxxxxx xx xxxx xxx xxxxxxxx xxxxx              │
        │   x xxxx xx xxxx xxxxxx xxxxx xxx xxxxxx           │
        │   xxxxx xxx                                        │
        │                                                   │
        │   ooo ooooooo                                     │
        │   xxx xx xxxx xx xxxxx xxxxx xxxxx xx x            │
        │   xxxx xxxxx xxx xxx xxxxx xx x x xxxx             │
        │   xxxxx xx x xxxx xxxxx x xxxx xxxx xxxx           │
        │   xxxxxxx xxxxx xxxxx xx x xxxx xxxx               │
        │   xxx xxxxx xx x xxxx xxxxx xx xxxx xx x           │
        │                                                   │
        │   ooooooooo oooo                                  │
        │   xxxxxxx xxxx xxx xxxx xxx xxxx xxx xxxxx         │
        │   xxxxx xx xxx xxxxx xxxxxx xxxxxxxx               │
        │   xxx xxxx xx xxx xxxxxx xxxxxxx xx                │
        │   xxxxxxxxx xxxx xxxxxxxx xxxx xxxxx               │
        │   xxxxxxx xxxx xxxxx xxx xxx xxx xxx               │
        │   xxxx xxxxxx xx xxxxxxxx xx xxxxxxxx              │
        └───────────────────────────────────────────────────┘
```

Break information down into small information chunks and signal those chunks by leaving extra space between the chunks (sentences or paragraphs). Information may be structured by visually associating it in chunks. Those chunks of information are reinforced by grouping each together and separating them from each other.

```
            You should have generated
            a research hypothesis that
            resembles this one.

    NULL    There will be no difference in
HYPOTHESIS  concept identification between
            tutored and untutored children.
            ------------------------------

            Do you think that you could
            design an experiment to test
            this hypothesis?
```

Highlight important information. In the previous example, the term "Null Hypothesis" is highlighted, which directs the attention of the learner to that information. Highlighting may be done by underlining, using inverse or flashing text, different color text, all-capital letters, italicized letters, and so on. The information to which attention is directed will be better remembered. Be careful not to highlight too much information.

Provide a map of the content with the current location highlighted. Make it available as an option so learners can clearly see where they are located in the course or lesson. In addition to knowledge of content, learners must also possess structural knowledge (knowledge of the interrelationships of the ideas or concepts in a lesson) in order to fully comprehend the material. The idea of a cognitive map was discussed in part 1 and in the concept learning chapter in part 2. This type of map will illustrate the structure of the content.

Use unit bridges to structure content. This simple but effective device is used when there are units or sublessons that follow the first unit of a lesson. Each following unit should have a bridge screen at its beginning. This bridge is a screen that refers to the content of the previous unit/lesson and relates it to the new one:

```
        In the last unit you
        learned how to define
        and select hypotheses.

        In this unit you will
        learn how to test your
        hypothesis, to see if
        it solves the problem.
```

These unit bridges are especially important when the learner may finish one unit of the lesson one day, and return to the next one on another. It is an effective device to recall prior knowledge and prepare the learner for new knowledge, as discussed in chapter 2.

Organize the screen into functional areas. Display a specific kind of information or activity consistently in each area. The ultimate form of organized screen display is to break the screen up into specific areas. The following examples show the top line being used for content orientation (name of the lesson or sub-lesson, screen number, concept being studied, etc.), the bottom line showing the options available to the learner (e.g., exit, answer, glossary, help, feedback); above that are a line of directions about what the learner is to do next, an area in the middle for displaying text information and graphics, and an area in which the learner may make responses. If the system allows use of windows, the windows are excellent means for presenting this kind of structured information. Rather than chopping up the screen, the user can simply open a window to get the needed information.

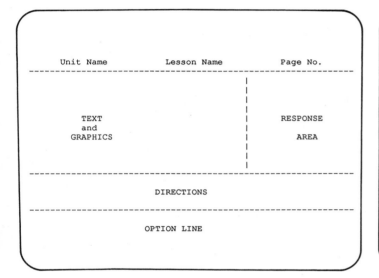

Designing Simple
Screens

While providing structural information, keep in mind that simple screen displays are more easily comprehended than overcrowded displays. While structure and simplicity may seem in conflict, they really are not. Screen displays need to represent a compromise between the two. The examples in the second principle below are simple screens (displayed in notational format).

Use only one-third to one-half of the total screen capacity in any display. If the screen can display 24 lines of 48 characters, 960 characters or spaces are available. Use no more than 488 of them, and preferably less. Somewhere between 320 and 450 will best display a simple screen.

Double-spaced text is easier to read and provides a simpler presentation. The examples below, using the notation method again, show simple screens. Too much information can distract the learner. Dense text is hard to read.

```
          oooooo  ooooo  oo  oooooo

       xx x xxxx xxxx xx xxx x xxxx xx x

    xxxxxxxx xx xxxx xxx xxxxxxxx xxxxx

    xxxx xxx xxxxxxxxx xxxx xxxxxx x xxxxx

    xxxxx xxx

    ooooo oooo oo ooooo ooo

       xxx xxxxx xxxxxxxx xx xxxxxx

    xxxx xxxxxx xxx xxx xxxxx xx x xxx

    xxxxxxxx xxxxxxx xxxxx xx x xxxx x xxx

    xxxxxxxxx xxxx xxxxxx xxxxx xxxx xx

       xxxx xxx xxxx xxx xxxx xxx xxxxx

    xxxxx xx xxx xxxxx xxxxxx xxxxx

    xxxxxxxxxxxxxx
```

Designing Spacious
Screens

Another important feature of well-designed screens is spaciousness. This is more related to simplicity because simple screens are usually spacious. Generally, make ample use of white space or black space or whatever the background color is. One of the virtues of computer displays is that it does not cost more to use lots of extra screens to present the same amount of information. With print materials, extra space results in extra paper costs. In CAI, space is essentially free, so keep screens spacious.

For spaciousness, use 40-60-column text rather than 80-column. In 40-column mode, the letters are larger and the spaces between the letters is greater, producing a more spacious appearance. In the examples below, the appearance of the screen is very spacious.

```
┌──────────────────────────────────────┐
│ oo ooooooooo  oooooo ooo  oooooooooooo    ii │
│ xx     x xx     x xx     xxx xxxxxxxx │
└──────────────────────────────────────┘

 ooooo ooooooooo ooo oooo

    xx x xxxx xxxx xx xxx x xxxx xx x

 xxxx xxxxx xx xxx xxxxxxxxx xxxxxxx

 xxxxx xxx

 ooooo oooo oo ooooo ooo

    xxx xxxxx xxxxxxxx xx xxxxxx

 xxxx xxxxxx xxx xxx xxxxx xx x xxx

 xxxxxxxx xxxxxxx xxxxx xx x xxxx x xxx

 xxxxxxxxx xxxx xxxxxx xxxxx xxxx xx
```

```
 ooooo ooooooooo oooo        xx xxxx xx xxx x xxxx xx x

                            xxxx xxx xxxx xxx xxxx xxx xxxxx

                            xxxx xx xxx xxxxx xxxxxxx xxxxxxx

                            xxxxx xx xxx xxxxx xxxxxx xxxxx

                            xxxxx xxx

 ooooo oooo oo               xxx xxxx xxxxxxx xx xxxxxx

 oooooooooo                  xxx xxxxxxx xxxx xxxxx xxxxx xx x

                            xxxxx xx x xxxx xxxx x xxxx xxxx xxxx

                            xxxxxx xxxx xxxx xxxx xxxxxxxx xxxxx

                            xxx xxxxx xx x x xxxx xxxxx xxx xxx x xx

                            xcxxxxx xxxx xxxxxx xxxx xxxxxx xxxx

                            xxxxx xx xxx xxxx xxxxxx xxxxxxx
```

Double spacing text also increases the perception of spaciousness. The sample screens above both show double-spaced text. The side headings increase the sense of spaciousness.

Displaying Textual Information

The majority of information displayed in all forms of media, including CAI, is still text. Information is stored and retrieved in the form of text. CAI makes very heavy use of text to present information. So knowing how to display text is as important to the CAI designer as it is to the print page designer. Some text design principles that will improve display of text are presented below.

Text on the screen should be left justified—ragged right. When text is justified to the right margin so that both the right and left margins are smooth and even, the text on the line is expanded to fit the line, so that inter-word spaces are varied. This makes the text harder to read.

```
It is important that you remember the
formula 5F - 9C = 160. Try to think of
some jingle or mental picture that you
can attach to the formula, such as "the
5 Fords and 9 Chevys made a 160 degree
turn...," and/or an image of these cars
turning. These are memory tricks that can
help you remember the formula.
```

Left justified, Ragged right

```
It  is  important  that  you  remember  the
formula 5F - 9C = 160. Try to think of
some  jingle  or  mental  picture  that  you
can  attach  to  the  formula,  such  as  "the
5 Fords  and 9 Chevys  made  a 160 degree
turn...,"  and/or  an  image  of  these  cars
turning.  These  are  memory  tricks  that
can help you remember the formula.
```

Right justified (uneven spaces)

Only titles should be centered. Text which is centered (center-justified) so that both the right and left margins vary equally is hard to read.

```
It is important that you remember the
formula 5F - 9C = 160. Try to think of
some jingle or mental picture that you
can attach to the formula, such as "the
5 Fords and 9 Chevys made a 160 degree
turn...," and/or an image of these cars
turning. These are memory tricks that can
help you remember the formula.
```

Centered text is more difficult to read

Do not use hyphens to break words on the screen at the end of a line. Continuation in reading is harder on the screen than it is on a print page of text.

Use a typeface (if there is a choice) which has full descenders. Descenders are the tails in letters like g, y, and p that extend down below the line. It is easier to read words made up of letters with descenders than a lot of computer-generated type which does not use descenders.

Use lowercase text in presenting information. Computer-generated text is often uppercase only. This is more difficult to read than lowercase (with uppercase for capital letters where appropriate).

Highlighting of text should be used consistently. If using a certain type of highlighting (e.g., inverse text, different color text) for directing attention to certain words, be certain to use that form of highlighting consistently. For example, if the display is normally white type on a sky-blue background (one of the best combinations) and green text will be used to highlight those words which appear in the glossary, make certain that green text is not used for any other purpose. Use a different form of highlighting for signaling headings, for instance.

Use no more than three forms of highlighting at any one time. Too many signaling systems will only confuse the learner. For example, use green text to signal glossary words, underline the critical attributes of a concept such as reinforcement, and use capitals for headings. That is enough!

Using Color in Screen Displays

A distinct advantage of computer-generated displays is the ease of painting the screen in vivid colors. Avoid the temptation to over-color the displays. Too many colors is distracting and can confuse the learner.

Use the brightest colors for the most important information. The greater the contrast, the more obvious information will be. Avoid the consistent use of very high contrast information, such as white type on a black screen. The excess contrast can cause eye strain and fatigue in the learner.

Use no more than three or four colors on any single screen. Too many colors on the screen can be distracting to learners.

Use colors consistently to signal certain information. Like directing devices, the use of color to signal certain functions or information should be consistent. For instance, if there is a blue background behind the text portion and a green background behind the response part of the screen, do not use those colors on any other portion of the screen for any other purpose.

Use neutral colors for the background. Colors such as light blue, grey, light green, and other neutrals make good background colors on computer screens. They reduce the contrast that causes eye fatigue, and they do not distract the reader.

Message Design

Probably the most difficult part of creating CAI or any computer software is in designing clear messages or directions that will not be misinterpreted by users. It is much more challenging than may be apparent. For example, designers at Apple Computer had to write six different revisions to an on-screen question about whether a user of a piece of their software was actually using a color display monitor. A seemingly simple question. After six revisions, they were able to get the error rate in using the software down to a tolerable level. The best test of the message design is, of course, to try out the software or portions of the software with users who are representative of the target population.

Directions should be stated in short, action-oriented sentences. In giving directions or asking questions, state them in terms of what the users will do or should be doing.

When users are required to perform a sequence of activities, number the activities in the proper sequence. Use short, action-oriented directions: Do this, Now do this, then do this....

```
            PROCEDURE FOR PERFORMING
                SALAMI PRINCIPLE
-----------------------------------------

In order to schedule your activities using
the SALAMI PRINCIPLE, you should do the
following things in this sequence:

1   Think of a large scale daily task.

2   Slice the task into small bites.

3   Estimate the time you will need to
    complete each.

4   Find a time in your daily schedule for
    each bite.
```

Never use the passive voice in presenting directions, options, or information. Do not say, "It should be done." Rather, say "Do this."

When using conditional statements, state only one condition and one consequence and signal those as clearly as possible. Conditionals are the hardest type of information to convey to the general public. Most people have a hard time with contingent operations. So it is important to make the condition and the consequence as obvious as possible.

```
If this is the first time that you have
run this program,

Then press the "N" key.
```

```
                IF          |        THEN
------------------- - -------------------
                            |
you want to store a |  press "K" and "D"
computer program    |  keys simultaneously
                            |
------------------- - -------------------
                            |
you want to load a  |  press "K" and "L"
computer program    |  keys simultaneously
                            |
------------------- - -------------------
```

Planning Screens

In this final section, we present a few aids and tips for helping to pull instructional design, lesson design, and screen design together.

Using a Planning Guide

Before sitting down in front of the computer to load BASIC or Pascal or Pilot or C or your favorite authoring system, or anything, for that matter, you need to plan what each display or screen will look like. Coding the program from the instructional design will cause objectivity and intent to be filtered by the language being used. In dealing with the editors, the syntax and programming conventions, you will forget all about most of the screen principles that you just learned. Just getting something onto the screen will be sufficient reward for your efforts. You are the designer and may be planning to give your designs to the programmer to convert into computer code. In either case, you should use a planning guide to help develop a meaningful lesson and later communicate your instructional intent to yourself or to the programmer. The general sequence for planning the lessons and screens is presented below and reflects the order and structure of this book.

Identify the instructional goals and objectives, classify those goals, and determine the instructional events necessary for instructing those lessons. You should have accomplished these by now. You have learned to prepare verbal learning lessons, concept lessons, rule lessons, and problem solving lessons. Make a list of each of the verbal learning, concept, rule and problem solving segments required to get the learner to accomplish the objective. Do this for each objective. Next, determine the sequence in which these segments will be presented or whether the learner will control the choices. From this information, sketch out a map of the lesson segments or create an outline (such as the one done in part 1) of the lesson segments. This is the content structure from which you can create the content orientation line at the top of each screen.

Determine the lesson components needed for each lesson and sub-lesson. For each lesson component, you must decide how to display the information, ask the question, elicit the behavior, or otherwise communicate your instructional intent. Identify the basic information needed to display the component, as you did in the chapters in part 2. Next, decide how that information is best displayed. From this process, make a list of operations, activities, functions, or options that the learner will use to get through the lesson (e.g., help screens, menus, etc.). This options list will help you to structure the general screen and deciding what options to list on the program options line.

Convert the lesson components to screen displays. For each activity, you must now create the text, graphics, instructions, menus, and so on. On copies of the screen design guide on the next page, first add the content and functions lines and then sketch in the text or graphics. Play with the design. After creating the first few screens, glance back over the principles in this chapter for any gross violations of the principles. If there are violations, try to think of good reasons for them. If there are not any, revise the design a bit. Be certain that to number the screens and indicate the screen numbers that this screen leads to as well as the screen numbers that lead to it. This will be extremely important when assembling the program.

Code the screen displays into a program. The designer may do this or a programmer may. If the screen directions are clear enough, the programmer should have no problem.

Appendix

Sample Screen Display
Sheets

Unit: _____   From: _____

Frame: _____   Next: _____

<u>Problem 4</u>   Back: _____

        Mr. Talbot rewards Nicole with a gold star when
        she turns in a neat paper. Soon, every paper
        she turns in is neatly written.

        This is an example of:

        (a) Positive reinforcement
        (b) Negative reinforcement
        (c) Premack principle
        (d) Punishment
        (e) Extinction

****

<u>CA</u>:   (a) Right! Nicole's behavior has been changed via a
            reward given. Let's try another one.

<u>Try 1</u>:   W1 > (b) No, the behavior is leading to a reward being
            given, not an adverse consequence being avoided. Try
            again.

            W2 > (c) No, the reward is external to the person, not
            an activity enjoyed by her. Try again.

            W3 > (d) or (e) No, the behavior is getting stronger,
            not weaker. Try again.

            ELSE > No, you did not type in A, B, or C. Try again.

<u>Try 2</u>:   (not a) No, the answer is "A." <u>Positive reinforcement</u>
            is a procedure in which a reward external to the person
            is presented in order to strengthen a behavior. (Level
            1 help: definition re-stated)

Programmer Instructions: _____
_____
_____

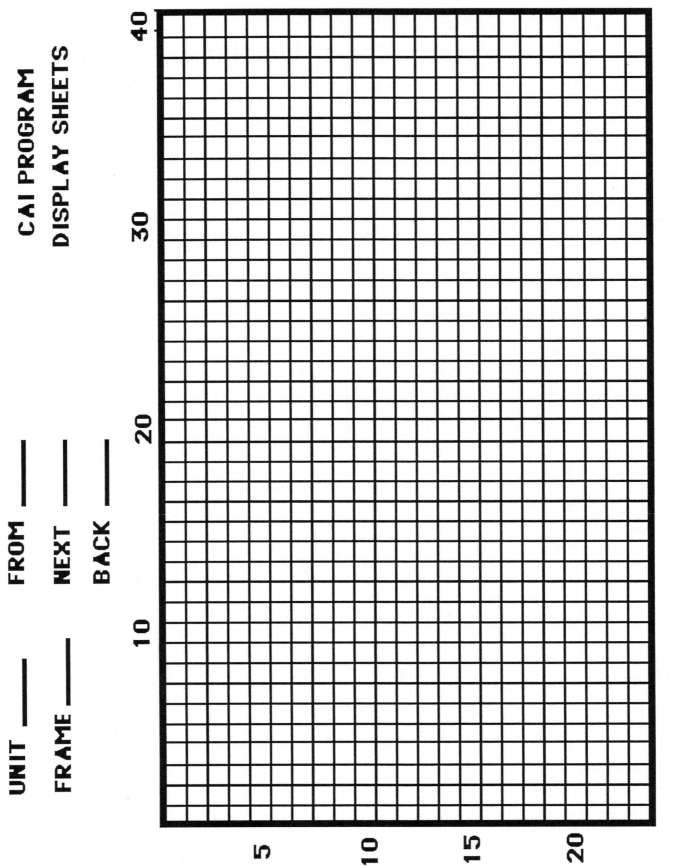

CAI PROGRAM
DISPLAY SHEETS

UNIT ——
FRAME ——

FROM ——
NEXT ——
BACK ——

INSTRUCTIONS TO PROGRAMMER : ——

CAI PROGRAM

DISPLAY SHEETS

UNIT _1 - PERCENTAGES_   FROM _4_

FRAME _5_   NEXT _6_

BACK _4_

```
NOW, KNOWING THAT ELWAY THREW 40
PASSES AND COMPLETED ONLY 5,
WHAT PERCENTAGE OF PASSES WERE
COMPLETED?

        a) 11.0

        b) 12.5

        c) 25.0

        d) 50.0

PRESS THE LETTER OF THE CORRECT
ANSWER, THEN HIT RETURN
```

INSTRUCTIONS TO PROGRAMMER: _____(NEXT SHEET)

Accept as correct : B or b or b) or B) or **12.5**

Correct 1st time >   "Great job! Let's try another."
   " 2nd time >   "Good job! Let's go on."   ⟩ Go to frame 6.
   " 3rd time >   "There you go."

Incorrect 1st time >   "Try again."

   Hint: "What fraction of his passes were completed?"

   " 2nd time >   "Try again."   ⟩ Go to frame 4.

   Hint: "What is 5/40?"

   " 3rd time >   "Incorrect. Let's move on.   ⟩ Go to frame 6.
                  The correct answer was B (12.5)."

Selected Bibliography

Instructional Design

Dick, W., & Carey, L. (1985). *The systematic design of instruction* (2nd edition). Glenview, Ill.: Scott, Foresman & Company.
Contains good explanations and examples of learning outcomes, learning analysis, objectives, and lesson strategies.

Gagné, R. M., Briggs, L. J., & Wager, W. (1988). *Principles of instructional design* (3rd edition). New York: Holt, Rinehart & Winston.
A little more complex than the Dick and Carey book, but has more in-depth coverage of learning outcomes and learning analysis.

Kemp, J. (1985). *The instructional process*. New York: Harper & Row.
Clear explanation of steps and features of instructional design.

Design of Computer-Assisted Instruction

Alessi, S., & Trollip, S. (1985). *Computer-based instruction: Methods and development*. Englewood Cliffs, N.J.: Prentice-Hall.
Good book for more knowledge about computer games, simulations, drills, and tests.

Hannafin, M., & Peck, K. (1988). *The design, development, and evaluation of instructional software*. New York: Macmillan & Co.
As its name implies, this book treats all three phases of CAI, and includes the learning theory behind effective software. A popular college text.

Jonassen, D. (Ed.). 1988. *Instructional designs for microcomputer courseware*. Hillsdale, N.J.: Lawrence Erlbaum Associates.
Fine collection of readings on different aspects of instructional software, including drills, feedback, tutoring, and authoring systems.

Kearsley, G., & Halley, R. (1985). *Designing interactive software*. La Jolla, Calif.: Park Row Press.
Short, well-written book that describes the essentials of good screen design, user control, and response analysis. Good chapter on how to promote interactivity through branching.

Sternberg, E. R. (1984). *Teaching computers to teach*. Hillsdale, N.J.: Lawrence Erlbaum & Associates.
Informative book on how to use effective instructional features in computer software.

Simulations and Games

Loftus, G. R., & Loftus, E. F. (1983). *Mind at play: The psychology of video games*. New York: Basic Books.
Discusses attentional and motivational features of computer/video games.

Malone, T. W. (1981). What makes computer games fun? *Byte*, 6, *12*, 258-277.
Discusses motivational/instructional features of computer games.

Reynolds, A., & Martin, J. (1988). Designing an educational computer game: guidelines that work. *Educational Technology*, 28, *1*, 45-47.
Basic how-to's of game design.

Rowe, N. C. (1984). Some rules for good simulations. In Walker, D., & Hess, R. *Instructional software: Principles and perspectives for design and use*. Belmont, Calif.: Wadsworth Publishing Co., 181-185.
Contains some of the basic how-to principles of simulation design.

Tutorials

Ross, S. M. (1984). Matching the lesson to the student: Alternative adaptive designs for individualized learning systems. *Journal of Computer-Based Instruction*, 11, 42-47.
Describes methods for "personalizing" computer-based instruction to make it more effective.

Drill and Practice

Salisbury, D. (1988). Effective drill and practice strategies. In Jonassen, D. (Ed.). *Instructional designs for microcomputer courseware*. Hillsdale, N.J.: Lawrence Erlbaum & Associates, 103-123.
Excellent article about how to design and develop a sophisticated drill and practice program.

Salisbury, D., Richards, B., & Klein, J. (1985). Designing practice: A review of prescriptions and recommendations from instructional design theories. *Journal of Instructional Development*, 8, *4*, 9-15.
Contains a number of learning outcomes-based prescriptions on how to improve drill and practice programs.

Weyh, J., & Crook, J. (1988). CAI drill and practice: Is it really that bad? *Academic Computing*, 2, *7*, 32-36ff.
Describes a drill and practice program for the sciences that embodies many effective drill and practice features.

Evaluating CAI Courseware

Miller, S. K. (1987). *Selecting and implementing educational software*. Boston: Allyn & Bacon.
Contains a number of criteria and guidelines for evaluating CAI software.

Truett, C., & Gillespie, L. (1984). *Choosing educational software: A buyer's guide.* Littleton, Colo.: Libraries Unlimited.
Informative text on methods and criteria for evaluating CAI programs of all types.

Zemke, R. (1984). Evaluating computer-assisted instruction: The good, the bad, and the ugly. *Training*, 21, *6*, 22-47.
Entertaining and informative guide to software evaluation.

Screen Design

Hermes, J. M. (1984). *Screen design strategies for computer-assisted instruction.* Bedford, Mass.: Digital Press.
In-depth look at the tools and procedures for planning CAI via screen displays.

Learning Strategies

Jonassen, D. (1988). Integrating learning strategies into courseware to facilitate deeper processing. In Jonassen, D. (Ed.). *Instructional designs for microcomputer courseware.* Hillsdale, N.J.: Lawrence Erlbaum & Associates, 151-183.
Elaborates upon methods of using learning strategies in computer courseware.

Index